be/come COMMUNITY

JAMES B. ASHBROOK

Judson Press, Valley Forge

BE/COME COMMUNITY

© H. W. Richardson 1971
Judson Press, Valley Forge, Pa. 19481

Many quotations from the Bible found in the text are the author's
own translations and paraphrases. Other versions which have been
quoted as noted in the text are as follows:
   The Revised Standard Version of the Bible, copyright © 1946 and
1952 by the Division of Christian Education of the National Council
of the Churches of Christ in the United States of America, and are
used by permission.
   New Testament in Modern English. © J. B. Phillips, 1958. Used by
permission of the Macmillan Company and Geoffrey Bles, Ltd.
   The Jerusalem Bible. Copyright Doubleday and Company, Inc.., 1966.

This book is a curriculum resource developed by the American Baptist
Board of Education and Publication in cooperation with the Christian
Church (Disciples of Christ), the Church of the Brethren, and the Church
of God (Anderson, Indiana).

ISBN 0-8170-0438-6
Library of Congress Catalog Card No. 70-107654

Printed in the U.S.A.

preface

This book is to be experienced
as much as it is to be read.
It <u>can</u> be read as you normally
read — that is, assume letters
add up to words, words add up
to concepts. If it is thus read,
you will get part of what I am
saying. Yet you will be bewil-
dered by seeming disruption of
usual expectations and ordinary
experience.

One thing is certain: this book
will take some getting used to.
Therefore it <u>cannot</u> be read in
your regular way if you would
get its full meaning.

Because it does not restrict itself to what you anticipate, you
will experience unusual reactions. You may well confront strong
emotions welling up — uncomfortableness, anger, hostility, resentment at "being toyed with." You may unexpectedly experience mounting enchantment — curiosity, excitement, fascina-
tion, de**light** with "seeing."

Do not give up trying to read as you usually do. But do not rest content with the familiar. Press on, puzzling as it may seem at first, to less common sorts of meanings.

To find other meanings sometimes may require you
 — to read a sentence or a section aloud
 — to let your eyes "see" the page differently
 — to allow your mind to

w a n d e r   where it will

 — to talk about the book with someone else.
Keep open to what comes.

Because of your unique way of experiencing the world, there is always more than a single meaning. Don't be afraid of the meaning you see. Mine isn't the only one nor even the most illuminating one.

Soon you may discover you are seeing and experiencing the WORLD in fresh and freeing ways.

table of contents

from a theological point of view

it is best to avoid
the word "Church"
as much as possible,
if not altogether.

At all events,
this overshadowed and overburdened word
should be immediately and consistently
interpreted by the word

"COMMUNITY." [1]

Karl Barth

Where are you?

Genesis 3:9 (RSV)

1

what is the situation? ambiguity

The stereo blares. The beat beats. The words cry:

I am a rock, I am an island,
and a rock feels no pain
and an island never cries.[2]

Friendship hurts. Love bruises. I am "a fortress
deep and mighty that none may penetrate" [2]
—I protect myself against the crush of others.
Is that true? Does friendship hurt? Can love bruise? Are relationships harmful? Who can say for another? Who can say for
oneself?

When I feel strong and am simultaneously close to
others, nothing is more undesirable than being a rock and an
island. When I feel uncertain and am simultaneously cut off
from others, an island is inviting and a rock seems desirable.
In strength I connect. In weakness I flee.

C?u*t/o%f#f$ or c-o-n-n-e-c-t-e-d?

Who wants to be cut off? Do you? I don't. I want

to-be-tied-in with life. I want to be part of what matters. I want
to be alive to life. When I am not moving into life, I am thereby
moving out of life.

[2] From "I Am a Rock" by Paul Simon. © 1965 Charing Cross Music.
Used with permission of the publisher.

Yet we do see   m   iss c(o4n2n1e0c@t%i*n#g.
to

SomehOW we do not always tOUCH. At times our senses fAIL to function. . . . We do not really see; we do not really hear; we do not really understand (Matthew 13:13-15) . We get c?u*t//// o%f#f$ through IGNORancE and insENsitiVitY (Ephesians 4:18) — cut off from each other, cut off from ourselves, cut off from meaning, cut off from God. We get cut off ●   Then we cannot   ?

Apparently, a way of being born and becoming genuinely human lies embedded in recovering our sensitIve-NESS (1 Peter 1:23) . When we can see and hear and understand, then

we are alive,
we make connections,
we are inspired!

By now you must be wondering: What has gone wrong? Has the typesetter fallen asleep? Has the writer lost his senses?

Ordinarily we think every experience has only one meaning. We anticipate the familiar and we find what we expect — that is, as long as life flows smoothly. But life cannot be contained and life is not contained. Again and again and again, Spirit breaks up structures that life might live. Then, while anticipating the familiar, we bump into the unexpected.

If we stay with the unexpected, we find depths of meaning enriching previous experience. If we struggle with the strange, we grow in our ability to be responsible stewards of God's creation (Genesis 1:26-30) . Whether struggling with the elusiveness of this book bears any necessary relationship with becoming responsible stewards is an open question. But to grasp various sorts of meaning does bear a necessary relationship to participating in the creating-redeeming-sustaining activity of God.

As a clue to understanding less familiar sorts of meaning in this book, refer to the top of this page. You will discover that it hurts when we do not touch. We cry "OUCH." You will see that being cut off by ignorance and apathy demands that we give up destructive comparisons. We are to "IGNORE ENVY." You will learn that sensitiveness requires an heightened sense of "I-NESS" — that is, knowing who I am in relation to where I am and to what is happening <u>to</u> me and <u>through</u> me.

When we claim the Word became flesh and dwelt among us (John 1:14), emphasis shifts from abstract words <u>about</u> God to experienced reality <u>of</u> God. In the jargon of contemporary communication, "the medium is the message." [3] The content of the message and the way the message comes aCROSS are the same REALity. What we say and how we say It make the same impACT. The <u>what</u> expresses the <u>how</u> and the <u>how</u> discloses the <u>what</u>.

The marriage of the message-and-the-medium is a verbal/nonverbal form of communication. Look back again on page 10. You will notice when I suggest we seem to miss connecting, the very way the letters, spaces, words, and images are set down conveys the message nonverbally: "We do see m   iss c(o4n2n1eOc@t%i*n#g." Yet I trust that God takes
     to
this nonverbal method and uses it according to his purpose.

With this orientation, we can pick-up the thREAD of awakening sensitIve-NESS in order to be/come human community.

According to the creation story in the book of Genesis, man's eyes were opened when hebumpedinto another human being. The instant he sensed another person he experienced distance between himself   and   the rest of creation. Connections b

      r
       o
        k
         e
    •   down. Anxiety flooded in. His eyes

widened

His heart beat faster faster fasterfasterfaster. The environment threatened. The Creator deMANded, "Get-with-it."

GenesIS is not so much past history as present experience. We miss Its impACT (!!) if we simply relegate it to the dawn of history. The story is about us — human beings — you and me and everyone. It describes inner truth in terms of outer events. It points to the insENsitiVitY of being (c%ut## o*f"f(((and to the possibility of reestablishing c-o-n-n-e-c-t-i-o-n.

Adam does not mean "a man" as James Ashbrook is a man. Rather the word implies "man" or "mankind." I am Adam! You are Adam! Everyone is Adam! Adam is everyone!

Similarly, Eve does not mean "a woman" like my wife. Rather the word implies "life" or "mother of every living thing." This is my living! This is your living! This is our living!

Creation in GenesIS means creating every living reality. The story of Adam and Eve, therefore, opens up the uneasy awareness that goes with our "getting-with-it." In that moment God addresses us:

Adam, where are you?
What is the truth of your situation?

Mankind, where are you?
What is the truth of your situation?

MAN, WHERE ARE YOU?
WHAT IS THE TRUTH OF YOUR SITUATION?

If we start anywhere but where we are personally, we m s connecting. So let's start with that which is most immediate i s and most real — the experience of ourselves: your experience of yourself, my experience of myself, and the in-betweenness that is ours.

WHERE ARE **YOU?**

Do not go racing ahead to find some answer from me. I cannot tell you where you are. Only you can. So stop reading. Give up second guessing. Simply and directly, can you say what it's like where you are?

What's around you: space? crowdedness? things? people? problems? possibilities? Much in our environment we perceive only dimly. We tend to block out the unpleasant and the challenging. You will find you have to work consciously at sensing the effects the various parts of your world have on you. How do you see where you live? What impressions **sweep** past you on the way to work? What gets **through** from the media?

Where are you in your life space — your standing ground — your place in the world? Do you have a place that is you? Can you move freely and easily — within the home? at work? in play? through the country? within humanity? Are you displaced or misplaced? Is your space comfortable or uncomfortable? Full of life or drained of life? Do you feel openness or emptiness? chaos or carefulness? What is **your** space like?

Where are you in relation to

The question is not about time of day or year. That's lifeless information. Where are you in the time of your life — the meaning of your moments? Do you feel time running out? standing still? dragging its heels? racing ahead? pregnant with possibilities? What time is it for you?

What do you see? Close your eyes for 30 seconds: allow the images lurking in the background to emerge. What comes? What is going on? Where have you gone? What are you doing?

What interferes with your being here conversing with me in this book? Does my style bother you? Do I fail to communicate? Or does something else pull you away? When you leave the here-and-now, where do you go? Return to the past? Race ahead toward the future? What unfinished situations clamor for your attention? You may find the images that appear reflect the experiences pulling you away from the present.

By now I hope you are seeing more clearly, hearing more keenly, and responding more fully. In short, I hope you are more able to be where you are when you're there. Only by such heightened sensitIve-**NESS** do we understand what it means to have-to-be-in-this-world. And by standing (under) what is we participate in becoming.

Where we are as individuals is intimately entangled with where the world is. Even when we want to be islands and rocks, we find ourselves connected to a now-and-here more than ourselves. The words we use, the clothes we wear, the food we eat, the understandings we receive — all remind us we are children of the time and place in which we live.

As we begin to sense where we are, so we begin to ask:

WHERE IS THE WORLD?

Humanity as a whole asks the same jolting question we ask as individuals: "World, where are you? What is your situation?" Every kind of person shouts that question — black, white, brown, student, teacher, moderate, militant, leader, led, young, old — everyone.

In the mid-sixties we heard "The Times, They Are A-Changin'." That was not a new theme, yet it conveyed a new tempo. Everything isspeedingupspeedingupspeedingupspeeding up. . . . .

A third grader struggles with her homework. Her all-knowing, all-wise ninth grade brother tells her what to do. She informs him, "Things have changed since you were in third grade!" That retort witnesses to accelerating times.

A few minutes later her first grade sister expounds on two kinds of producers and two kinds of consumers in the American economy. That baffles the third grader. She has never heard of "consumers" and "producers." What does "economy" mean? How did she miss out?

Eventually, the first grader consoles her with the prospect, "That's all right. You'll get it when you go to college." One minute the third grader acts superior; the next, her confidence collapses. New curricula get newer every year.

What took generations to change now pops out between grades. We live in the age of the instantaneous. We know who wins elections before the polls close. The lag between an idea (minutes/hours/days/weeks/months/years) and its implementation vanishes

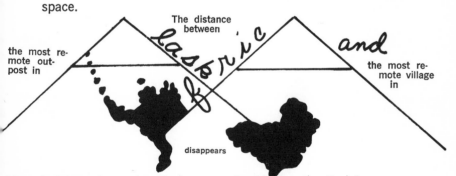

The popular tune fades "out" almost before it sweeps "in." Information often travels faster from the other side of the globe than from the other side of the office.

Instantaneous time is matched by simultaneous space.

Via television-telstar, the Alaskan and the African, the Parisian and the New Yorker watch the same game at the same time. Lunch in Paris — indigestion in New York.

In 1965, Harvey Cox provided fresh images to help us understand our time of transition. He painted the WORLD as The Secular City. He celebrated its liberties and invited us to its discipline. His telephone switchboard concept accentuated the meaning of our anonymity. Only those who had our number got through to us. His emphasis upon cloverleaf underscored the meaning of our mobility. People on the move upset the status quo. They sought the new, the different, the novel. They accepted the strange, the foreign, the unusual.

In contrast, one year earlier, in 1964, Marshall McLuhan announced the electronic age has transported the wOrLD back into the stage of being one big, overgrown, tribal village. Through the Kennedy/King/Kennedy assassinations the television set made us one aching family — no longer simply anonymous people always on the move. In an expanding universe we are jammed onto a contracting planet. Once we sprawled into many places; now we congregate in a sINgle place. Once we could live apart; now/we/live/continuously/together. The electronic media have broken through our switchboard anonymity. Technology has replaced the mobile novelty of the cloverleaf. "In the electric age," declares McLuhan, "we wear all mankind as our skin." [4]

The celebration of the city, however, tumbled with eruption in the ghetto. The pleasant white world shuddered from black power and brown power. Everyone learned that no group is all good or all bad — that each group is a rumbling conglomeration. Black is beautiful/ugly even as white and brown are. White is militant/moderate even as brown and black are. Brown is sensational/comfortable even as black and white are. The city is promise/peril even as rurban is peril/promise.

Yes, "the times, they are a-changin' " but they are a-changin' every direction. From rural-to-urban. From city-to-village. From togetherness-to-separateness. From the personal-to-the-corporate. From speed up-to-slow down. From participant-to-observer. From spectator-to-actor. From there-to-here. From then-to-now. And back again. Everything is different. Everything is the saME.   Yes; no.   No; yes.

Research[5] sharpens these impressions. In American CULTure, the following changes in values have emerged:

"being and becoming"	vs.	merely "doing"
the "present time" and the immediate	vs.	the "future time" and the distant
"aesthetic and recreational values"	vs.	duty and drudgery
EXPRESSION	vs.	suppression
release	vs.	repression

other directedness   VS.   inner directedness
rely on one another   VS.   rely on oneself
living with and for and through OTHERS

a prizing of some kinds of TOLERANCE and diversity
While conformity increases in small groups, variety
multiplies among groups. There is less dogmatism,
less moralism, less fanatical insistence upon one
pattern, one truth, one way, one view.

a drift toward an EQUALIZATION OF THE ROLES
OF MEN AND WOMEN. Women are moving into
the mainstream of the working force. Long-haired
men and short-haired women confuse the unobservant.
Women reject the role of homemaker for the task of
personhood. They want to be persons in their
own right. "I'm me before and besides being
a wife, a mother, a teacher, a secretary, a
          , a   , and a   !"
Where is the world? Who can say? All we know is

that we are $b_o{}_{un}c{}^{in}ga{}_{r}{}_{ou}n{}^{di}{}_{n}$the Age of Endless **Reversi-
bility.** Reason becomes unreasonable and the unreasonable
reasonable. Beauty masks terror and terror discloses beauty.
Imagination constricts to technology and technology releases
imagination. War is peace and peace war. Freedom is slavery
and slavery freedom. West identifies with East and East mirrors
ʇƨɘW. Nothing stays put. Everything swings.

Yet we can stand under the endless **ytilibisreveR** and
the surprising reverberations with confidence. Within the world
is the WORD (Genesis 1:1; John 1:1). Within the WORLD is the word.
Within the **WORLD** is the WORD!!!

And where is Community in this instantaneous, simultaneous, **gnisrever,** swinging world?

COMMUNITY, WHERE ARE YOU?

WHAT IS YOUR SITUATION?

One institution claims to be Community.
That is the church! What is happening to it?
Ferment within the church (community) matches ferment within the world. Since the end of World War II, we have
re   al,
grown giddy with the taste of new wine: renewal,   new
new   n wa
re   al, re e   l. In some places the new wine was poured into
old wineskins. Predictably: churches split, denominations
rocked, seminaries sweated. In other places the wine flowed
into new wineskins. UNEXPECTEDLY:
small groups
HARDENED INTO little cLIquES
storefronts
ORGANIZED INTO eStablIshmeNts
advances
MEANT retrEATS
The Church Inside Out [6] in mission to the world became little
more than the outside in in catering to itself.
The Americanization of the God of Abraham, the
God of Isaac, and the God of Jacob grew more obvious.[7] Class
replaced faith. Religious identification and social position
tended to describe the same phenomena, only with different
labels.[8]
Catholics and Jews were Democrats; White
Protestants were Republicans.
White Protestants were most likely to
believe in the American dream; Catholics and Negro Protestants were least
likely to.
Jews were most likely to favor the welfare state;
White Protestants were least likely to.
Those who were the most devout tended
to be less prejudiced than those who
were devout sporadically.
The Age of ytilibisreveR characterizes the church
even as it does the world. P o p e   J o h n   X X I I I   t h r e w   o p e n
t h e   w i n d o w s   o f   R o m a n   C a t h o l i c i s m .   T h e
w i n d s   o f   t h e   W O R L D   f r e s h e n e d   i t s   a t m o s p h e r e ,
w h i l e   fanning the flames of its conflicts. Pope

Paul VI burned up authority by reclaiming the authority of rhythm.

Protestantism acknowledged authority and organization by tightening its lines of	connections. The ordering of its life and thought re- duced chaos,	while suffo- cating the li-	fe of Spirit.

To ask "what is the situation?" is to reel under the impact of conflicting answers. Even though the camera stops, the action jets ahead. Generalizations are possible but misleading. Specifics are misleading yet possible.

Where I am — where you are — where the world is — where community (church) is — can only be described in kaleidoscopic images. Not only do each of us see the situation differently but even we ourselves see differently at different times. We see, we organize, we interpret in an infinite variety of ways. What seems to be the same objectively always carries within it the interaction between itself and its obSERVER. And that means varying meanings.

Linus' response to the situation can never replace Charlie Brown's. Sensitlve-**NESS** depends upon their unique experiences as well as the shape of the clouds. In addition, their responses are shaped by Charlie's sense of inadequacy in the presence of Linus' confidence and of Lucy's demanding-ness.

We are aware of and at**tend** to what we anticipate. We anticipate what is familiar. The more we need to experience specific situations, the greater our ten**den**cy to overlook other elements in the situation. We **tend** to seek what is pleasant and to avoid what is unpleasant. We respond to what interests us and ignore what di**STUrBS** us.

Yet, in periods of reversal and up h e a v al the times are out-of-joint. To be unaware of or insensitive to the situation is to court disaster. The issue is not whether or how much we are disjointed. Rather the issue is: how are connections re-established?

We begin by hearing the **quest**ion **of Genesis**

WHERE ARE YOU?
WHAT IS THE SITUATION?
In answering that **QUEST**ion, we may yet come to our senses and recover our c-o-n-n-e-c-t-i-o-n-s. Then

our eyes see
our ears hear
our hearts understand

<u>and</u>   we

respond!

He led captivity captive.
Ephesians 4:8 (Phillips)

2

boxed-in and breaking-out

• • •
• • •
• • •

What do you make of these dots?

Probably nothing! But stay with them for a bit. How would you describe "the situation" of the dots? Would you say there are three rows of three or three columns of three? Would you say there is a box with a dot in the middle? What do you say is "there"?

There are a number of ways to describe the dots. In order to describe them, however, we have to make certain assumptions. Somewhat arbitrarily I have labelled them "dots." I could have said "circles," especially if they were magnified, or "pinpoints," especially if they were minified. I could have shifted the focus by asking, "What do you make of the white spaces?" As soon as I said "dot," though, the possibilities of what you saw took shape in a way that both focused and restricted what you saw.

Research on what we see-and-remember suggests the problem of focusing and restricting possibilities. Two groups of people were shown a series of simple yet ambiguous pictures. Before seeing its particular picture, each group was given a different word supposedly describing what they were about to see. After being shown the picture, they were asked to draw what they saw. The samples below demonstrate how the "actual" picture was modified in the direction of what each group expected to see.[9]

"Actual" figure	Group I		Group II	
	Word list	Reproduced figure	Word list	Reproduced figure
	Curtains in a window		Diamond in a rectangle	
	Bottle		Stirrup	
	Ship's wheel		Sun	
	Two		Eight	

Remember

    the word is not what we see
    the word is not what we see
    the word is not what we see!

The word only points toward what we see. As soon as we think the word is what we see, we limit the possibility of seeing what may be there. For instance, when we "see" Viet Cong, we may start thinking "enemy" and forget thinking "persons."

Return now to whatever was at the beginning of the chapter. Can you connect all nine dots with four straight lines without lifting your pencil or retracing any line? Try it and see. Remember: include all dots; draw no more than four straight lines.

Unless you are unusual you are experiencing some frustration. "Nine dots with only four lines? It's impossible!" I suspect you are feeling foolish and impatient with my nonsense. The exercise has boxed-you-in. Probably you can neither do what I suggest nor forget it. I have blocked your thinking and cramped your attention. But do not let me dissuade you. Keep trying. Remember: nine dots; four lines.

What you may be experiencing touches upon a common experience. We get the sense of being boxed-in. Everything is so tight we can't move.Elbow room has disappeared.MAYBE

your home traps you

your neighborhood traps you **your color traps you**

your job traps you

time runs *out*

Being boxed-in takes many forms. It is blind, deaf Helen Keller saying, "I feel sometimes as if I were a music box with all the play shut up inside me." [10] It is war ⌊war?⌋ ▮war! that no one knows how we got in and no one knows how we get out. It is racism and repression and resentment. It is being overwhelmed by rage or lust or longing or desperation. It is being imprisoned in our own attitudes, our own reactions, our own imaginings. Four lines cannot connect nine dots! Regardless of its form, whether political or economic or social, the box represents all that corrupts and cripples and curtails becoming genuinely human.

Fortunately, we do not always feel boxed-in. Sometimes we discover we

My home frees me

I am loved and I love!

My work frees me!

I am necessary!

Though

I am changed

I respond

What are we to make of these contrasting experiences? A clue may be found in a series of events that went something like this:

A scattered group of Semitic nomads
found themselves working
as slaves for Egyptian Pharaohs.

They were abandoned, forgotten, overlooked.
The world's justice passed them by.
They were boxed-in.

Somehow, by a strange combination of circumstances, they found themselves delivered.

They were remembered.
They had broken-out.
They discovered they were a people!

What did that mean? One moment they were slaves; another they are free. One moment they were a motley collection of riffraff; another they are welded together as a people. One moment they were boxed-in; another they have broken-out.

PEOPLE BREAK-OUT

On their own they realized they had neither the strength nor the leadership to break-out. They were slaves and they knew it. Almost any negative word described them: weak, cowardly, fickle, timid, irresponsible, unreliable, skittish, wayward. By themselves they were nothing. They presented no "body" solid enough to stand out as living humanity. On the surface their experience added up to being boxed-in. Nine dots cannot be connected by four lines.

Yet they had broken-out. No "body" now stood out as God's "body" (1 Peter 2:10). Four lines can connect nine dots.

In the experience of Moses, the no-people-become-people found their clue. What at first made no sense, on deeper reflection made much sense. What is that clue?

In the wilderness of Midian, Moses collided with unexpected reality. While tending sheep, he saw a bush that burned without burning up. What did that mean? Moses wanted a word label to understand. By what name shall inexhaustible reality be called (Exodus 3:13)? What confronted Moses?

Not dissimilarly Robert Frost described his confrontation with a star: [11]

O Star (the fairest one in sight),
. . . to be wholly taciturn
In your reserve is not allowed.
Say something to us we can learn
By heart and when alone repeat.
Say something!

Like Moses and like each of us, Frost demanded a word — a label — a response in order to make sense of the experience.

. . . And it says "I burn."

Being. Existence. Somehow that is not enough.

But say with what degree of heat.
Talk Fahrenheit, talk Centigrade.
Use language we can comprehend.
Tell us what elements you blend.

Such endless questioning brings no reply — only the first and basic answer, "I burn."

It gives us strangely little aid,
But does tell something in the end.

. . .

It asks of us a certain height,
So when at times the mob is swayed
To carry praise or blame too far,
We may choose something like a star
To stay our minds on and be staid.

Bush, star, cradle, cross. "I exist. And because I exist you, too, exist."

Yahweh — Lord — Jehovah — that was the given name. That was the mystery clue. To Identify reality — to know the nAMe — to be sensitized to the event — was to enter Into contACT with the Other.

No name;   No relationship;

no relationship.   no understanding.

The word — the name — the reality — God — say something! [12]

I am
I am that I am

I am here
I am here, really present,
ready to help

I cause to be
I cause to be what comes into being

I will be what I will be. . . .

YHWH. Unlike a thing that has reached its final form, here was Nameless Name — the "name of four letters" and no vowels — "living process." [13] Previously, whatever worked at freeing individuals and groups bore another label than YHWH.

I appeared to Abraham, Isaac, and Jacob
as God Almighty,
but by my name YHWH
I did not make myself known
to them. (Exodus 6:2-3)

Now, however, the breaking-out reality that is and causes and creates and frees became known in a coming together of what seemed like accidental and isolated experience. With what was Moses confronted in Nameless Name? Could we say he was face-to-face with Love (1 John 4:7-8)? Why Love? Because Love gives without exhausting itself. Love gives without perishing. Love can be pictured as fire and flame and passion. Love sets men's hearts ablaze (Luke 24:32). Such is the nature of caring possibility. No experience, however overwhelming, can finally displace Love (1 Corinthians 13:8-10).

No information was given about what degree of love. No information was given about what kind of justice. Only the summons: Live;   break-out of every box!

I have seen
the affliction of my people . . . in Egypt,
and have heard their cry . . .

I know their sufferings,
and I have come down to deliver them
out of the hand of the Egyptians,
       and to bring them up out of
       that land
       to a good and broad land . . .
       (EXODUS 3:7-8).

Here lay the clue to understanding Inexhaustible Reality. I AM (Exodus 3:14) comes with experiences of people breaking-out of boxes. God does not abandon people. He acts to destroy oppression. HE summons EVERyONE — you, me, the world, the community (church) — to freedom and accountability.

To the onlooker, the escape of a handful of ghetto slaves from egypt-inner-city-europe-suburbia-america-office-asia-home-africa-church-organization simply marks part of the endless shifting of population throughout history. Egyptian records bypassed it in silence, although those did mention a class of seminomadic people known as Habiru. That a small band of slaves got away hardly caused a ripple. Even the Hebrews themselves saw NOthing of SIGNificance. Again and again they argued for the security of egypt in contrast to the uncertainty of the wilderness (Exodus 16:2-3; 17:3-7) .

Yet to some participants, and especially Moses, the break-out carries deep personal-universal significance. Life's meaning opens up.

FREEING RELATEDNESS

For these people, the break-out does not fade into a museum piece. For them break-out is a present reality. Today, 3200 years later, Jewish families celebrate this event as their event. The passover meal (Exodus 12:8) is also a feast of unleavened bread,[14] which was used to expedite the escape. It is the duty of the celebrants to imagine they themselves have come forth out of egypt.

The son asks the father, "What does this
                            ceremony mean?"
The father answers the son,
"It is because of what the LORD (YHWH) did for me

when I came out of egypt.''

(Deuteronomy 6:20-25;
Exodus 12:21-28)

Because of the egyptian break-out, we can see what is happening with new eyes.

Because I AM, you can be.
Be/cause YOU ARE, you be.

Live. Respond. Answer. Literally, the break-out depends upon seeing the situation as other than a box.

Recall the nine dots and four lines. Probably you have been struggling with that configuration as a box. As long as you do, the task is impossible. Re-image the situation. Re-define what is there. Loosen your grip on the given. Think of an arrow in flight. Instead of a static-trapped actuality, imagine a moving-traveling possibility:

Wherever break-out occurs, the same I AM is at work!

A RESPONDING COMMUNITY

Even so, break-out is never an end in itself. An unchecked ex PANSION of POSSI-BILITY Leaves

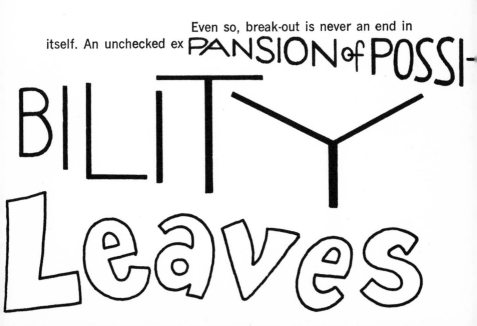

An endless expansion of possibility balloons into nothing! The purpose of break-out is more genuine humanness.

The egyptian escape makes possible a new community for a new humanity. It lays the foundation for a reorganization of life. People see the world differently. Like the Freedom Movement giving Black People a new experience of being, those who have never belonged to anyone now find **THEM-SELVES** belonging to some**ONE**. Those who have been no people now experience themselves as BEING's people. The experience begins with escape; it climaxes with demand (Exodus 20:1-20; 21:1ff; 34:1–35:9).

At Mount Sinai nobody-now-somebody enters into a relationship of trust and responsibility, accountability and answerability with I AM reality. They get together. They enter into covenant. They understand

YOU ARE, therefore,
be/come COMMUNITY

They find new ground for their life in the world.

As a result, every thought and act are seen in terms of the nine-dot arrow of becoming genuine human community. I AM breaks us out in order for us to become as he intends. No life remains unrelated and unrelatable.

Thus in the book of Exodus we find long discussions of how the unrelating-now-relating people are to order their lives. There are regulations about stealing, cursing, coveting, farming, and real estate. There are regulations about borrowing, sacrificing, courtesy to strangers, and telling the truth. To see only isolated dots unrelated to the attitude and character of relatedness is to remain boxed-in. To see the directional arrow is to b r e a k - o u t . A straight relationship with BEING necessitates straight relationships with others. Straight relationships with others mirror a straight relationship with I AM.

The break-out people of Israel, and later the breaking-out people of "I have made your I AM known" (John 17:6, 26). are "hope made visible." Four straight lines can connect nine dots. It has happened. It does happen. It continues to happen!

We are summoned to dignity.[15] We are answerable for the situation in which we find ourselves. We are to forge new relationships. The some-bodies created by I AM are re-sponding-bodies. Relationship entails responsibility.

> I AM frees us;
> WE ARE frees others.
>
> I EXIST says something;
> WE EXIST says more.

Inexhaustible Reality does not go **AWOL** on us; we are not to go **AWOL** on others. Inexhaustible Reality cares with us; we are to care with others. When we look at the endless detail in **EXODUS**, we are to see organizing-for-genuine-human-community-in-this-world.

As Egyptian-escape is a sign of BEING's break-out power, so Sinai-demands are a sign of WE ARE's responding-body.

HUMAN MEANS

I AM says quite clearly:

I have seen . . .
I have heard . . .

So come, I will send you—that **YOU you YOU you You YOU**
that **you you YOU you you You**

may bring I AM's people out of egypt . . . . . .
(Exodus 3:7-10).

The break-out activity of I WILL BE is ever and al-ways and forever tied with YOU and ME and US and BODY and PEOPLE and COMMUNITY. God humanizes through hu-man beings. God "genuinizes" through human means. Nine dots are not connected by four lines apart from your and my and our acting on the possibility.

The no-possibility-for-the-world becomes genuine hu-man-possibility-for-the-world through reorganizing dots and lines from boxes into arrows. I AM/COMEs through personal and social change. Whenever no-bodies are CALLED PEOPLE, Loving Care burns inexhaustibly. Be/cause I AM, YOU ARE!

See that group of 8- and 9-year-olds playing.[16] The girl with the needle has not seen her father in two years. She misses him. Life grows lifeless. Break-out contracts into a box □. A needle pricks her finger. Not much. Just a little. It hurts. It huRTS. It HURTS! IT HURTS!! IT HURTS ! !!

IT HURTS

What hurts? Finger? Hand? Heart? Life?

IT HURTS! LET ME GO I NEED MY
MOTHERFATHERNEIGHBORBROTHERGODLOVE

Perhaps it isn't just your finger hurting. Perhaps something inside hurts.

MY FATHER WENT AWAY
I DON'T HAVE a daddy.
HE neveR cOmes hOMe,
I NEED MY daddy.

She stood very close and cried. In the midst of the tears a 9-year-old came and put her I AM around I HURT.

      I don't have a daddy either.

      My parents are divorced.

      My father is far away.

The two I HURTs stood close to each other.

I AM + YOU ARE = BREAK-OUT

That is how Inexhaustible-Caring-Reality works. We each know what it is to be  . Along with that we also know **BREAK OUT**. Another — YOU ARE — PEOPLE — COMMUNITY comes over and puts its **I AM** around our i am <u>not</u>. By such answering-responsibility we participate in Inexhaustible Humanizing.

By the new and living way which he opened for us.

Hebrews 10:20 (RSV)

3
in-the-way and making-way

Words get-in-the-way. They stop
us from moving around. Sometimes
words carry such deep emotional staining we can only see
      Fundamentalist — red flag!
      Liberal — red flag!
      Humanist — red flag!
      Church — red flag! red flag! red flag!
      Christ — green light —
          and his church — red flag! red flag!
      Love — green light — green light — green light —
          green light
      Religion — red flag! red flag! red flag!

Other words neither trigger resistance nor awaken
agreement. We simply take them as they come. Still other
words arouse our interest. They stimulate us *TO RUSH FORWARD*
      The same inhibiting or freeing effect applies to ob-
jects of interest. When we see something intriguing, our 👁 👁

OPEN to take more in. When we see something dis-
tasteful, our eyes close to shut it out. We tend to be more open
to some experiences and less open to other experiences.

Words, people, institutions, situations seldom exist apart from their personal meaning. What opens my eyes may shut your eyes and what shuts my eyes may leave you **wide-eyed**. The more personal words-people-institutions-situations are, the less casual our response. To the degree they get-in-the-way, to that degree they stop us. To the degree they make-way, to that degree they aid us.

Religion is one such personal word. It stands for any and all <u>organized</u> faith as well as for any and every <u>personal</u> meaning. Consequently, for some, religion stands out. For others, RELIGION shrinks away. For a few, religion appears like other words.

I confess I have never felt comfortable with the word. I see RELIGION as well as religion. For me, as for many, RELIG ON implies that which destroys life.

Yet I also acknowledge I have never felt comfortable without religion. I meet in it sensitivity to dimensions of

personal hurt often missed by conventional concerns — loneliness, estrangement, destructiveness, arrogance, blindness, tragedy. . . .

social injustice often entrenched and ignored by the majority — an inferior status for women, invisibility for minorities, poverty from sameness, conventionality, and conformity . . .

I experience religion confronting and encountering that which is most disruptive <u>and</u> most creative.

Even more unexpectedly, I discover denominational and ecumenical structures encouraging the most freedom for getting around in the world. I know religious advocates to be among the most genuine, the most real, the most alive, the most in-touch. When so many RELIGIOUS people get-in-the-way of humanness, these others are making-way for humanness.

Herein lies the dilemma: RELIG ON gets-in-the-way and destroys life; religion makes-way and affirms life. As those called to a new and living way, we are faced with a high view of religious **reality** and a low view of religious expression. Nowhere is that portrayed more sharply than in the Letter to the Hebrew Christians. <u>Hebrews</u> floods us with churchly expression — the shedding of blood, priestly rites, perfect sacrifice. Its architecture of the universe is absurd — a shadowy, unreal, temporary, elusive first floor with a permanent, perfect, real second story. No wonder the nineteenth century philosopher Søren Kierkegaard complained, ". . . there is a strange, stuffy atmosphere which we encounter in Christianity. . . ." [17]

At the same time <u>Hebrews</u> cuts through sham and pretense. It exposes the real and the vibrant. Its radically radical approach

accentuates the universal longing for direct access
to that which heals brokenness

rejects busyness that
only reinforces failure

recognizes that real
change is costly

insists upon the utter
reality of Jesus
as
the pioneer
of
possibility.

Consider the contrast between expression (words, activity, organization) that must be rejected and reality (language, persons, organ-ization) that can be affirmed:

EXPRESSIONS THAT
GET-IN-THE-WAY

"In this outer tent," claims the author, "we see a picture of the present" religious

expression

(Hebrews 9:1-10, Phillips). These expressions hinder our becoming genuine human community:

   a holy place — a sanctuary furnished with
                 fixed symbols of divine mystery;
   a holy priest — a mediator carrying out
                 activity on our behalf;
  a holy sacrifice — an offering making up for
                 our failure in obedience.

These, we are warned, destroy life. These, we are informed, cannot "possibly bring any worshipper to perfection in his inner self"(Hebrews 9:9, Jerusalem Bible). These, we find out, cannot restore genuineness. These are shown up in their true light as getting-in-the-way!

what is wrong with a holy place?

Does not I AM HERE have a right to a place? How can he be known without a grounding- a location? Did we not learn in breaking-out BEING requires a body?

A "Body" without a place is no-body at all!

The time has come!

What time has come?

The time has come not to celebrate what matters in special places neither out-of-doors nor indoors (John 4:19-21).

What are you talking about? What are we supposed to do?

"You are I have made your I AM known" John 17: 6,26

Celebrate inexhaustible reality in spirit and IN trUth (John 4:23-24)!
Celebrate "because I AM, you are" spONtaneousLY, uncalculatINgly, perSONally, corporately!
Celebrate "because I AM HERE, you are becoming" withoUt fanfARE, wiTHOUt propagANDizIng!
No place in-spires; only I am living!

No place fulfills; only I AM HERE!
There is no-body except "I have made
your I AM known" (John 17:6, 26)!

A holy place grounds BEING in an arbitrary setting
with arbitrary symbols and arbITrary doings. We remain emo-
tionally fixated on an "edifice complex." If only we build the
right building, then people fINd **GOD**. The temple of the Lord
— the temple of the Lord — the temple of the Lord — the
temple of the Lord — the temple of the Lord — the temple
(Jeremiah 7:4).

Despite the presence. of the living Word, we dash
into "activity neurosis." If only we do something, then SomethINg happens. Committeescommitteescommitteescommittees
meetingsmeetings
meetingsprograms
programsprograms
goingconcerngoing
concerngoingconce
— "a hive of little bees with the due proportion of drones and
stings." [18]

We fal
l
i
n
t
o
t
h
"conTENT illusion." If only we give
enough information, then there is LIfE.

John 3:16 John 3:
16 John 3:16 John
3:16 2 Corinthians 5:
17-18 2 Corinthians
5:17-18 2 Corinthia
ns 5:17-18 1 Peter
2:5 1 Peter 2:5 1 P
eter 2:5 1 Peter 2:

What is that **NUMB**er a**GAIN**?

What is wrong with a **HOLY** pl**ACE**? The mathematics
of living space are not what relig ous people think they are.
"A house is not a home." Genuine community does not equal
special space!

Surely nothing
is wrong with
a holy Priest?
Does not God require
someone who knows
his name and can
make him known?
How can he be
understood without
a go-between?
We cannot recognize
him without help

The veil of the temple
is torn in two (Luke 23:45)!

What do you mean?

The veil dividing what is
available to people and what is accessible
only to priest. The holy of holies — the place of the very
presence of the most high — open **ONLY TO** the set-apart-

MakEr-known — and to him only once a year — is now Opened

— exposed to all — for all time, for black/brown/yellow/white.
A holy priest perpetuates the block between ordinary
people ███ and ███ extraordinary PriEsT. ███ He ███
plays the part. ███ He ███ carries out the RELIG ous
role. By having "the professional good man," ordinary people
— us, you, me, everyone except ███ PriEsT mInister ███
— ███ are **FREED FROM** perSONal responsibility for recog-
nizing, understanding and responding to BEING here.
He ███ does for us what ███ he ███ iNfORMS us
we cannot do for ourselves.
Does that last paragraph confuse you? Did you bump
up against those barriers? Were you annoyed? uncertain? irri-
tated? Did they make reading difficult? That is precisely the
point. When the minister as holy priest gets-in-the-way, nothing moves easily or effectively.
What is wrong with **A HOLY PriEsT?** The mathematics
of living (site [sic]) insight are not whatRELIGIOUSpeople think
they are. Genuine person does not equal special person.

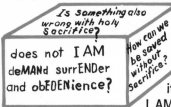

Is something also
wrong with holy
Sacrifice?

does not I AM
deMANd surrENDer
and obEDENience?

How can we
be saved
without
sacrifice?

Your
SAcriFicE-serVICE
it stinks (Jeremiah 3:2b; 16:5-18)
I AM sick (Isaiah 1:11-14)
I AM vomiting what you offer (Revelation 3:16)
He who does not love is dead. If you possess house,
car, savings, stock, charity, and in-sight into your brother's
(REALly **I AM**'s) need and bre$ak#c$ontac$t, how can
you say

Our father, who art in heaven . . . Our father, who art . . . Our father . . .

. . . religious deeds are all right, but <u>do</u> <u>not</u> neglect justice and mercy (Matthew 23:23).

The world is a beautiful place

to be born into

if you don't mind some people dying

all the time

or maybe only starving

some of the time

which isn't half so bad

if it isn't you.[19]

A substitute sacrifice rein**FORCES** worship with**OUT RE**new**AL.** Another does for us what only we can do for ourselves — live, breathe, trust, respond, give, receive, care, die. Every act of substitute worship-service symbolizes our dependence on others who tell us <u>that</u> we are guilty, <u>how</u> we are guilty, and <u>prescribe</u> ways to def**END US** against temptation.

Martin Luther attacked Roman ritual precisely on that basis. Its end**LESS** elaboration like an obsessiveobsessive obsessiveobsessivePRAYPRAYPRAYPRAYSINGSINGSINGSING WORKWORKWORKWORKcompulsioncompulsioncompulsioncom pulsioncompulsion, m**Ob**Il**Lize**S more anxiety by the very means it uses to control anxiety. When someone worship-serves for us, we remain spectators. When we remain **S**pect**ATo**rs, we leave worship-service unaffected. When we leave worship-service unaffected, we k**ILL** in-**SPIRIT**-ing.

What is wrong with **A HOLY SA**cri**FicE?** The mathematics of living (rite [sic]) right are not what ʀᴇʟɪɢɪous people think they are. Genuine living does not equal special sacrifice.

REALITY THAT MAKES-WAY

In rejecting religious expression the writer of Hebrews does not reject religious reality. Instead, he declares that now that Christ has come among us we have "a greater and more perfect tent which no human hand had made" (Hebrews 9:11, Phillips). He denies any desire to make one symbol, one group, one way of looking at the world absolute. He proclaims an authentically religious end to relig ▌ on:

instead of a holy place,
there is
a **PEOPLE** on the move;
instead of a holy priest,
there is
a genuine **PERSON**;
instead of a holy sacrifice,
there is
PARTICIPATION.

If religious expression requires a holy place, religious **REAL**ity discloses a witnessing **PEOPLE**. Life is never possession, only pilgrimage; never settledness, always search; never a roadblock, continuously a thruway. The po**TENT**ial of reality **DefIES** fixed representation: surprise, spontaneity, the unexpected, the unanticipated — these

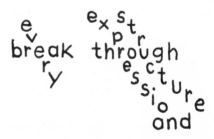

every break through expression and

Because community = PEOPLE-on-the-move instead of a place that stays put, every event poTENTially bears in-spiriting meaning. **NO REAL**m can be segregated as outside ultimate concern. We are freed to be in the

MIdST of the world (Galatians 5:1) as the body of Christ (Colossians 1:24b). While a house is not a home, there is no home without housing. While a place is not people, there is no people without place. The body is the place of the people.

The early days of the Freedom Movement dramatized part of what Church as witnessing PEOPLE-on-the-move means. During the Montgomery, Alabama, bus boycott, the Negro churches purchased a fleet of station wagons to transport people to work. Each was registered as the **PROPER**ty of a different **CHURCH**, the name of the sponsor being painted on the sides. These were "rolling churches," filled with people experiencing a new sense of who they were and where they were and what they were about. "Pedestrians who could find no room in the crowded vehicles waved as their own 'church' passed by, and walked on with new heart." [20]

A MOBILE PEOPLE makes-way for community. . . .

If religious expression demands a high priest, religious **REAL**ity discloses a genuine **HUMAN** being — not a role but a person. That which is human replaces that which is mechanical. As the early church father Irenaeus said of Jesus Christ, he became flesh and blood like we are that he might make us truly human like he himself is.[21]

The **SIGN**ificance of Christ's death opened-up

possibilities for our lives. In other words, that which is most central in our nature

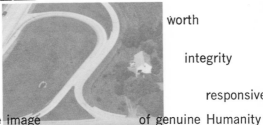

worth

integrity

responsiveness

creation in the image   of genuine Humanity

is supported by the basic fabric of life. We have direct access to centeredness. We need neither specific mediator nor specific time table. Authentic humanness has been built into

This is also not Community;

our hearts and structured into our minds (Jeremiah 31:31-34; Hebrews 10:16). We are freed from unloving and counterfeit pasts to live toward the future Hebrews 10:17-23; Ephesians 4:22-24; Philippians 3:13b-16). Each of us plays many roles — friend, spouse, worker, citizen, member, neighbor — but each of us is more than any single role or any sum of roles. Our central <u>human</u> qualities of trusting, responding, caring, and confirming break through every fixed role. The style of the way we come across sets the stamp of our humanity.

Through his flesh, Christ has opened for us "the new and living way" (Hebrews 10:20). Within each of us breathes the HUMAN.

REAL PEOPLE make-way for community. . . .

If religious expression demands a substitute sacrifice, religious REALity discloses personal PARTICIPATION. We offer our whole **i** am — feeling, thinking, intending — whether we give time, money, or ability (Romans 12:1).
We lose self-conSclousNess, reservations, our very identity in giving unconditionally to that in which we are engaged (Matthew 6:1-4). We are t**HERE**!

Personal participation necessitates being with what is happening. Instead of retreating to unfinished business in the past or *racing* *ahead* to unformed possibilities in the future (both of which destroy reality), we become **wholly** present. We do what we do when we are doing it. By emphasizing the rooted reality of what has been and looking forward to the hopeful possibilities that may be, we **SA**cri**F**ic**E** many possibilities f**OR** the sake of this **ACT**uality. **We are renewed to the degree we take part.** There are no proxies. There is no substitute. WE PARTICIPATE or

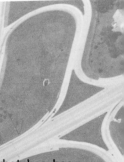

Frankly, I am uneasy about this immaculate division between **religion** and religion. Intended as a mortal blow to religious practice, the Letter to the Hebrews itself has been used as an instrument in its elaboration. No wonder many feel we should scrap religion altogether.

Nevertheless, I am equally uneasy without a genuine **religious** end to relig on, such as Hebrews exemplifies. A secular end to meaning that gets-in-the-way fails to make-way by itself.

Our world does not stand on its own feet. Meaning and direction are never self-evident. Love — loyalty — value — commitment come from beyond what is immediately at hand. They leap from what ought to be to what might be to what is. Ought to be lies within the truth of any situation but, like a mystery, remains unnoticed until we re**ORGANIZE** what we see in the light of what is de**MAN**ded. When we have only I ke-w th-I ke, we fall into the most serious deception of all — na**ME**ly, believing the WORLD to be only an extension of our under standing.

While experiences of
community relatedness
personal response-ability
fairness and justice
are rooted in every **CU**ltu**RE**, they stand in judgment on every **CULT**ure.

There and here we glimpse implicit **religious** pro**TEST** against that which makes our wor**L**d the final measure of everything that is. We see such traces in

the half-frustrated idealism of
Peace Corp veterans and student
slum teachers

the revolt against factory universities
teaching depersonalized subjects

the blacks' revolt against being
"invisible"; some whites' self-
transcending response[22]

Which way does the wind blow?

the "life is absurd" theme in art
and literature and politics.

Even the frantic fear of the radical right that the citizen has
become only a social security number in a collective machine
At**TEST**s to the criticism from beyond cu**LtURE** against culture.
Only an identification grounded in that which is more
than our own and other than our own prevents our being de-
voured by our own. Every protest derives its power of passionate commitment and its demand for honesty and justice
from that which is more than itself.

I look to **religion** that is more than

a mistress of the status quo
a rerun of old films

any single reality
the sum of several realities

I look to Jesus Christ
who breaks every mold in the power of new creation!

So then you are no longer strangers and sojourners,
but . . . fellow citizens with the saints
and members of the household of God.

Ephesians 2:19 (RSV)

4

out-of-touch and in-touch

Where there are no people, I WILL BE perishes!
Where there are people, I WILL BE parishes!
Without people no contact.
Without contact no communication.
Without communication no communion.

*In the quietness of a shared moment a
widower speaks of his wife and their relationship. "Irene, my wife, a remarkable
woman, we might have shared anything, and
yet, yet nothing in us combined, we could
not touch. She died in my arms, and at the
last I said, Are you happy, Irene? have I
made you happy? happy happy happy, those
were her last words: equivocal. I have never
understood whether she was saying yes, or
merely answering with an echo: I should
know if I'd ever known her."* [23]

*After the disastrous Bay of Pigs fiasco in
which the United States surreptitiously back-
ed an unsuccessful invasion of Cuba, President*

CHINA

John F. Kennedy told Arthur Schlesinger, Jr., of the part played by Allen Dulles, then head of the Central Intelligence Agency: "I probably made a mistake in keeping Allen Dulles on. It's not that Dulles is not a man of great ability, he is, but I have never worked with him and, therefore, I can't estimate his meaning when he tells me things.[24]

Our ability to comm**UNI**ca**TE** with each other pommels us with the most significant and perplexing f**ACT** of the **HUMAN** situation. Whether we look at intimate or global relationships, experience exposes isolation. We fail to understand.

The greater our confusion, the less our contact. The less our contact, the greater our confusion. Our different words and our several worlds fail to get across to each other.

white

Gap

the Affluent

HAVES

BLACK

STUDENTS

SECULAR

The Generation

Church

DEMOCRATS

the Poor

HAVE-NOTS

POLICE

REPUBLICANS

AMERICA

The Tower of Babel depicts that experience (Genesis 11:1-9). When we speak the same language, we need few words, for we are close. When we do not speak the same language, we need many words — you know what I mean, it's like, well, how can I put it exactly, somehow all my words

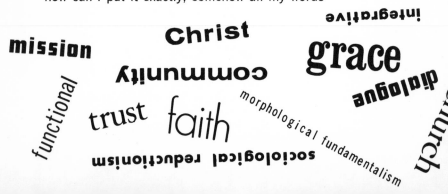

Christ

mission

grace

integrative

community

dialogue

functional

trust

faith

Church

morphological fundamentalism

sociological reductionism

empty phrases
empty phrases
empty phrases
empty phrases
empty phrases
empty phrases
empty phrases
empty phrases
empty phrases

theological reductionism God acceptance

sin

alienation organismic valuing

empty phrases pile up (Matthew 6:7), for we, you know, I mean you and I and the next guy, my neighbor, my fellow worker, those people on the other side of the globe, everyone, anyone, are physically close yet personally disTaNT. We mis stand under

mi stand
others and others **SUNDER** us.

Part of the confusion of tongues accrues from the fact no word says enough. Its meaning cannot stand out decisively. What, for instance, do I mean by the word "bridge"? Something that spans a chasm? A game? Dental work? Part of a nose? You cannot know unless I sharpen the context in which I am using the word. Words only point toward experience; words are never the experience itself.

Our different words and our several worlds hinder recognition of each other. Not seeing, we never touch. Not touching, we miss meeting.

Nevertheless, moments do occur when words speak and worlds meet. Suddenly, unexpectedly, at the very instant all contact seems gone, like a traveler in a foreign land, we chance upon someone who speaks our language — and we no longer feel helpless.

A word, a glance, a touch, a gesture, a contact, a meeting that declares
WE ARE IN-TOUCH . . . .

Widows of Violence

and when we are in-toUch, we shARE! And when WE shARE, we live! The in-spiriting power of the perSONal restores us to the land of the living.

When they — I mean, we — are gathered together in one place, tHERE comes a sound from EVERywHERE and NOWhere like the rushing of mighty wINd. And it fills the places of our parishing. Instead of our differences destroying relationship, they ignite Inexhaustible HUMANIZING — burning bush, tongues of fire.* Fullness not emptiness, life not loneliness, love not lostness, communication not babbling result . . .

> . . . filled with the Holy Spirit
> each speaking in different languages
> each hearing his own language
> (Acts 2:1-11).

"Holy Spirit" sounds so ghostly and unreal. Yet, if we take Pentecost as guide, In-Spiriting-whole turns out to be concrete, specific, personalizing. When the Spirit comes, we discover

> we can commUNIcaTE with others
> we are joined to a caring community
> we do let others know of breakthrough.

As the birthday of Community, Pentecost proclaims and celebrates what life is genuinely about.

There are moments — few for some, often for others — when we feel lonely, abandoned, out-of-place. Then from somewhere deep inside — in a way beyond our control yet in which we participate — the Spirit moves us. We let another see our hurt, share our loneliness, glimpse our out-of-placeness. The first tentative hint of hurt grows and grOWs and GROWS UNTIL clearly and directly we start talking —

I'M HURTING.
I NEED YOU.

I didn't know
Let's get together
YOU MEAN A LOT TO ME

You mean a lot
to me . . .

I WAS AFRAID you'd
make fun of me . . .

I was afraid, too.

I thought you were mad.

*The dove symbolizes the Holy Spirit being poured out as a free gift of God. It could also be interpreted as a flame, a burning presence that cannot be ignored.[25]

I GOT MAD be-
cause I didn't
want you to
know I hurt.
Nothing ever
bothers you.

If you only knew how much
agony I go through.

You're kidding?

I thought: If you knew I
was upset, you would feel
I was a weakling.

Weakling! You always
seem so superhuman.

If you only knew, if you only
knew, if you only knew. . . .

What a relief to find
you get upset just
like I do!!!!

you kn**OW** . . . yo**U KNOW** . . . you k**NOW**
I know . . . I know . . . I know . . .
NOW WE BOTH KNOW!

When we can say I instead of you or they or some . . .
When we can say explicitly what we mean instead of
"you ought to know without my having to tell you" . . .
When we can speak directly to the person we
want to get the message instead of to people
or everyone or anyone **. . .**
When we can specify the exact nature of the situation to which
we are referring instead of letting the other figure it out for
himself **. . .**
that is, when communication goes something like this:

"John, I thought you were ridiculing my
idea with your last comment. I felt 'Why
bother getting stamped on all the time!'
I have ideas but I can't seem to put
them into words as well as you can. I
wish you would give me time to say
what I have to say. If you take what I say
seriously, then I know you are taking me
seriously."

"When you just sit there and don't say anything, I feel you're mad at me. I wonder, 'What have I done this time?' I get to feeling more guilty and more upset and more shaky. Rather than ask what's going on, I get panicky. Then everything goes haywire."

"I don't need you to tell me whether what I'm saying is right or wrong or good or bad. I do need to know that you understand — really understand — what I'm trying to tell you. Maybe after I'm sure you do, then we can talk about what it might mean and what might be done."

Mere information nEVE*r inFORMS US about the kind of relationship we have. It may orient us in general; it never inspirits us in particular. Mere information never enables us to behold Inexhaustible Humanizing — the burning bush. Mere information never ignites the language of relationship — tongues of fire. Such breakthrough depends upon letting others know

> where we are,
>> who we are,
>>> what's happening,
>> what matters,
>>> what we intend and want.

When we use words and acts to disclose the true nature of contact, then our inner lives touch. We pass from ideas about life to living. We connect. Words and deeds get through. Communication sets the table for communion.

When in-spiriting awakens humanizing and establishes communication, we do not stop with simply getting through. Invariably, we continue BEING TOGETHER. We are joined to communing community. That is, we find ourselves in a pattern of relationships that support, strengthen, challenge, chasten, restore.

*Eve means "life"; cf. p. 12.

Although we know there can be contact without communion, we know equally that communion requires contact. Although we know there can be body without spirit, we know equally that Spirit must be bodied. Although we know there can be saying without meaning, we know equally that meaning necessitates saying. Although we know I AM HERE parishes in unexpected ways — a motley gang of runaway slaves — a backwoods carpenter executed for sedition — a quarreling band of cowards — we know equally that **HERE**ness and **NOW**ness show forth **AM**ness.

We learn what calls us from being nobody to be/come God's Body. We celebrate the break-out that makes way. We enter into others' worlds. We open ourselves to life. We respond to the word within WORLD. We intend uniting within comm**UNI**-ca**TING** (Acts 2:42).

Once basic connection gets communicated — in spite of words or acts or circumstances — we take up the task of making sense of New Being. **WE** sh**ARE** experience per**SON**-ally

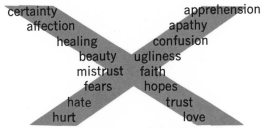

Instead of being "strangers and foreigners" we are "fellow-citizens with the saints" (Ephesians 2:19a, KJV). Despite the chaos of things, **HE**re **IS** homeland. We are not aliens in an alien world. We **BE**long **HERE**. This is our coun**TRY** — not a country with natural boundaries like the United States or the Soviet Union — but a hereness so vast and deep and broad no boundaries apply.

I WILL CAUSE TO BE gives us — the red, the brown, the black, the white — everyone without exception — this creation for <u>our</u> becoming (Genesis 1:27-31). What is around us and within us belongs to us — is here for us — is meant for us (Psalm 8:5-8)! If we receive connectedness (Romans 8:28), then facts are friendly.[26] We are joined to the whole f**AM**ily of man.

Instead of being "strangers and foreigners" we are fellow citizens . . . of the household of God (Ephesians 2:19b, KJV). The particular label applied to that Community of Acceptance is

unimportant. It has been called group, family, church, country. But the tag only tells <u>about</u> **BE**long**ING**; it <u>never is</u> the reality of belonging. We study the label to understand how to embody **I AM,** therefore, **YOU ARE.**

    I AM part of the body of NEW CREATION. We break bread; we seek meaning; we open ourselves to connections. A loving leisure pervades like delicate perfume. We let go of

BEING TOGETHER BEING TOGETHER BEING TOGETHER BEING TOGETHER BEING TOGE defensiveness — fearfulness — hiddenness — false pride — self-sufficiency — self-centeredness — and by so doing we are joined!

When being In-TOUCH overcomes being out-of-tOUCH, we find an inevitable development of experience. Initially, the message gets through: regardless of words and language you are connected. The relating WORLD is deeper than words about relating. The living Word calls us and draws us to others who also experience connections. We come together for enCOURAGEment, for underSTANDing and for identification WITH that which is more than ourselves.

The response, however, exposes how fully we do or do not receive-and-give the gift of In-TOUCHness. We are to test the spirit to see if it is of LETTING-BE or of MY BEING (1 John 4:1-3, 7-13) .

What happens to our connections beyond our tiny community of belonging marks the difference between life-spirit and death-spirit. If we funnel tenderness, love, understanding, care, communication only to ourselves and only to our own, darkness eclipses light (Amos 5:18-20) . To love only ourselves is to lose the very love we receive. A sign that the Spirit moves among us appears whenever we let others know:

BROKEN CONNECTIONS ARE REESTABLISHED!

As one person described to me her experience of lonely Babel and living Pentecost,

> "It's so strange, so intense, so weird. It's like being drunk, only alcohol can't get you this drunk. It happened in church [community ?? ! ! !] last Sunday. I didn't really hear what the minister said, only I was there. And I can't argue with that. That just is. There's no fighting something that is.
> "I have found quietness. I understand what the college professor was talking about when he spoke of agape—loving without strings and without lust. Really I have no words to describe what's happened. It's not a heady thing. Amazingly, the barriers are down. This love is something I have no right to hold on to nor keep to myself."

Having found, we let others know. We do not argue or fight or coerce or force them to k**NOW**. Rather we simply share life and loaf and love.

Perhaps
the great Russian
dancer Nijinsky caught
a sense of letting others
k**NOW**. In the last entry in
his "Diary" [27] before he died
he wrote:
My little girl is
singing: "Ah, ah, ah, ah!"
I do not understand its
meaning, but I feel what
she wants to say.

She wants to say every-
thing . . . is not hor-
ror

but

JOY

All things were created through him and for him. He is before all things, and in him all things hold together.

Colossians 1:16-17 (RSV)

5

cut-off and connected

Without you I cannot be.
Without me you cannot be.
Without each other
we do not become.

Now of course
these three sentences
exaggerate. Nonethe-
less, without some specific
and significant
person(s) in our lives
we cannot be human.
To eliminate you elimi-
nates me!

We are not made
to be alone (Genesis 2:18).
We are not people with-
out people. We do not
grow without others'
growth. Unless who I
am meets who you are,
we are both lost.

The biblical injunction to receive the other as a brother (Exodus 23:9; Leviticus 19:33-34; Philemon 15-16) is no arbitrary rule of etiquette. Not only have we been strangers in egypt, but in the stranger we discover unknown parts of ourselves. In receiving the (br)other we receive our very selves. In truth, we receive light and love and life (Matthew 25:31-46).

Yet much of our experience excludes the other. We cut-off those who differ. We avoid those who are different. The world divides into

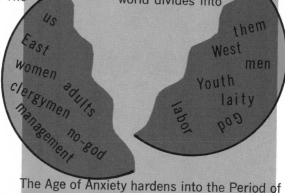

The Age of Anxiety hardens into the Period of Paralysis. Differences sever connections. Cut-off from a common world, we become locked into our several worlds. When we have only ourselves, there is **NO OTHER** conSIDEration.

In the situation where nothing holds together, all values grow relative; no value unites; all viewpoints are possible; no viewpoint reconciles. Unable to discuss, we end up unable to decide. Unable to decide, we find ourselves paralyzed. Without c-o-n-n-e-c-t-i-o-n there is only chaos. Then, no possibility is possible!

To be in the community-of-the-world implies that breaking-out and making-way and being in-touch are not ends in themselves. We are freed for more than ourselves. We are freed for others. But such connection with others comes slowly.

In the time of David and Solomon, Israel struggled with competing values: faith against faith, god against god, people against people, land against land. Whereas the faithful experienced that clash as destructive, an unknown prophetic writer informed them that the call to Abraham and the deliverance from Egypt were meant not just for ☐srael but for everyone (Genesis 12:1-3).[28]   I WILL CAUSE TO BE embodied israel as a sign — a declaration: **I AM deLIVerING EVERyone!** To those who rejected competing culture he pointed to common groUnd.

Years later (in the sixth century), during the ex-☐le, when becoming was again aborted, a deeper understanding emerged (Isaiah 40-55). With cities desolate, the temple ruined, and people in captivity, another unknown poetic prophet declared that Israel was to dramatize the fullness of faithfulness. Israel was not only a sign but a **LIGHT** — not for itself, but — for hu-**MAN**ity. To those who rejected enslaving culture he pointed to common groUnd.

Still the several worlds of "us" vs. "them" persisted. Revelation in nature — burning bush — shifted to revelation in history — exodus/exile — to revelation in a person — cradle/cross. Light-to-the-world became LIGHT-OF-THE-WORLD. In him we see what is **MeAN**t for all. In him we discover what is pre**SENT** in all. In him everything is related and relatable. In alpha and omega nothing remains obNOxious

For I AM is the ground of all; I CAUSE TO BE is in all; I WILL BE is before all; NAMELESS is the source of all.

Despite that vision of reality, the early church floundered from upheaval. A reckless freedom caroused outside the church, while limitless freedom erupted inside the church. An absence of shared customs, shared values, shared concerns meant the absence of shared society. Links broke that had previously held together. There was no common ground; only CONflicting valUes and comPETing loyalTIES.

In the midst of the paralysis, Paul reminded the church-as-Community of its connections (Colossians 1:16-17). Jesus-as-the-Christ is

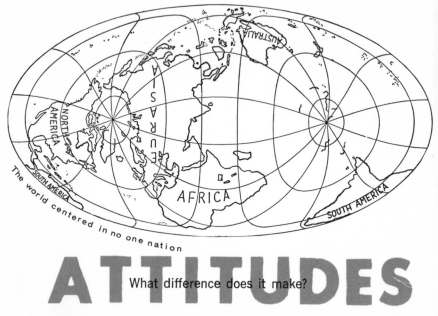

The world centered in no one nation

ATTITUDES

What difference does it make?

Because Christ is the ground and structure of the world, there are no intermediaries between us and reality. There are no go-betweens — not teachers nor preachers, not parents nor policemen, not whites nor blacks, not Communists nor capitalists, not religious nor nonreligious. Nothing and no one stands between any perSON or groUp AND the Impact of ultimate REALity.

Despite our particular values, common ground demands some kind of process by which we make value judgments. Christ as the ground and structure of the world makes possible significant value judgments beyond-yet-within comPETing values.

Despite our particular way of looking at life, common ground declares somehow we are able to comprehend life as life. Christ symbolizes the awareness of life itself beyond-yet-within conflicting sensitivities.

Paul also focused upon Christ as the c**ENTER** of the new creation — the living comm**UNITY.** As that ground, we are a people who participate in the key relatedness and potential relatableness of everything that is. Broken and distorted as the church (Community) (!) (?) (!) may be, that bodied Christ procl**AIM**s that

JESUS-AS-THE-CHRIST

<u>calls us to realize</u>   <u>frees us to participate in</u>
common ground   shared ground
in the created world   of the new creation
that <u>is</u>   that is <u>becoming</u>

No matter how self-sufficient we pretend to be, Christ confronts us with deeper closeness than we know. No matter how strange another culture may seem, Christ confronts us with the deepest cit**I**zen**S**hip of all. No matter how exclusively particular we assert we are, Christ confronts us with inclusive particularity.

I AM PARTICULAR

At the very moment all connections are gone, we know, we trust, we are convinced that when**EVER** we af**FIRM** the reality of common ground t**HERE** is

When **H☉PE** abounds

some possibilities are possible!

ACTIONS

What does it matter that "all holds together in him"?

Our life lies with others. The lives of others lie with us. Without that link we all are lost.

But what that link means is not self-evident. Connection is neither a single nor a static quality. It flows back and forth

b   then   a   now
 e t
   w   here   n   there
    e
     e
      n   no   d   yes.

ACTiON that carries out THE attitude of common HUMANity emerges as subtle and complex.

Move toward others

Without some movement toward contACT there are no connections. We must intend linking up. We must respond in ways that recognize the other's life situation as **hi s** and not as an extension of .
We must want to meet the (br)other.

I am an invisible man. No, I am not a s- pook. I am a man of	substan- ce, of flesh and bo- ne, fib- er and liquids — and I	might even be said to possess a mind. I am in- visible, underst-	and, sim- ply beca- use peop- le refuse to see me. . . . When they ap- proach me	they see only my surroun- dings, themsel- ves, or figments of their	imagin- ation — indeed, every- thing an- d any- thing ex- cept me.[29]

Unless there is open recognition we do not move toward each other. Whether whites or blacks, ministers or parishioners, parents or children, US or them ; without recognition we lack contact. We tend to SEE everyTHING except the living, hurting, hoping human being. Yet only by seeing each other as unique, do we move toward relationship.

As we stand with others in understanding, there come s **U**! dden, spontaneo **U** s, int **u** itive enco **u** nters. Then, I see see me! Our **i** 's meet — directly, openly, caringly, wordlessly.

But that intended movement toward others ought not to be taken casually. We need to ask ourselves: Do we really want to relate with others? Are we prepared to put ourselves at their disposal as Christ put himself at our/their disposal? Are we really prepared to show (agape) intelligent outgoing concern for others' well-being apart from our own? Are we prepared to be guided by the reality of others instead of playing with our own ideas of how they should be?

Do we — you — I — really want to be-for-others by being-with-others?

Move against others

Such closeness can dissolve into "sloppy agape." A sentimental gooing can sicken from the sweetness and complicate from the naivete. The consequence would be a suffocating intimacy, incest, ingrowness in which inherent weakness spreads because of the absence of outside influence.

The stand against others in understanding may be called confrontation. Endless growth is cancerous growth. It meets no resistance. It receives no counterbalances. It just goes on and on and on and on and on and on and on and on.

Confrontation stops whatever threatens to become un-**limit**ed *NO YES NO Self-expansion*

Such stopping constitutes negative feedback — information warning a person he is off course. He needs to refocus and reorganize what he is doing and who he is.

In moving against others we let them know what we see and experience. There will be differences, conflict, controversy. Yet each maintains his own integrity. Much of white confusion about black power arose because of white guilt and black fear.[30] Whites allowed blacks to stamp on them as blacks had allowed whites to do. Such giving up constitutes the worst form of disrespect — for oneself and for others. Respect refuses to buy what another sells — if in the process one's identity is destroyed and the other's   s extended beyond   its proper limit.

Detachment from the immediately obvious would be an undramatic way of saying what I mean. We care deeply to

see a situation in ways that make for arrows instead of boxes. There is a kind of de-<u>structuring</u> such as NAMELESS called Jeremiah to do — namely, to tear up, to break down, to shatter, to pull down in order to re-<u>structure</u> by building and planting (Jeremiah 1:10).

Recent biblical scholarship has uncovered a growth in understanding I AM — NAMELESS — KING. Israel did not find God to be the fulfiller of its best nor the protector of its lot. Instead Israel discovered YHWH "was different, over against them and especially over against their religion." [31]

When we move against others, we also allow others to move against us. We must encourage contrast and difference. We must accept controversy and conflict. No birth without pangs of birth; no resurrection without crucifixion. He who would save his life <u>will</u> lose it, but he who would lose his life for the sake of **REAL**ity <u>will</u> find it (Mark 8:35).

But that intended movement against others cannot be taken lightly. We need to ask ourselves: Are we strong enough to move against others? Are we able to face hard facts, risk anger, allow separateness, agonize alone in our own garden?

Are we able to stand firm in the face of others' failures? Are we able to be clear in the presence of others' frenzy? Do we have enough identity of our own that we are not downcast by others' depression, sucked in by others' dependency, frightened by others' fears, nor destroyed by others' bitterness?

Can we — I — you — really be-for-others by being-<u>against</u>-others?

MOVE APART FROM OTHERS

C-o-n-n-e-c-t-i-o-n necessitates more than being-with-others in encounter. C-o-n-n-e-c-t-i-o-n requires more than be-ing-against-others in confrontation. It likewise demands being-apart-from-others in humility.

To insure life we must allow death. "For reproduction by natural birth, Christianity substituted participation in death. It admitted a breakdown, an intermission of faith, between generations. . . . By choosing a limit for his [Christ's] own genius, he showed that the spirit will return to others in due season as long as no one usurps it too long and too exclusively." [32]

    NAMELESS **WILL** be**COME** — **God** — erects a barrier against every human loyalty. Jesus sees our most dangerous enemies as those of our own house**HOLD** (Matthew 10:34-38). He is not protesting the worst in us but the best. As Reinhold Niebuhr once quipped: to play God means to become the devil to others.[33] We must pray constantly

forgive us our possessing
as we forgive
those who possess us.

    Our links with others are necessary for growth yet not sufficient for growth. Against the inertia that would have kept Abrah**AM** in Ur of the Chaldeans, I **WILL CAUSE TO BE** calls each person to **LEAVE BE**hind what he has k**NOW**n.

    We must sacrifice the worthwhile as well as the worthless (Genesis 11:31–12:1). We can only go so far ourselves. We can only be so much to others. There always comes a point where we must step aside. Moses could see the Promised Land yet others crossed over without him (Deuteronomy 34:1-9). Jesus showed forth **I AM** inexhaustible **HUMANIZING,** but unless he went away men would not receive the **STRENGTH**ener (John 16:7). Despite the best intentions, paternalism (whether of position or color) has always meant one person doing something for another person that that person could do and should do for himself.

    As **PAR**en**T**s, we m us t

stand aside
with our own
inner tear-
ing as we see five-year-OLD

strike off down the street for
school

sixteen-year-OLD
drivedrivedrivedrivedown
the street
with the liberating license

young adult
enter soberly yet naively
into marri**AGE**

⊔ ltimate g⊏⊐owth means moving apart from others. **WE** prepare the way, yet we are **NOT** the way. We are necessary yet never sufficient. In such relatedness I WILL CAUSE TO BEcome demands we limit life

interrupt   continuity

let go

give up

DiE

But that intended movement away from others cannot be taken carelessly. We need to ask: Are we humble enough for a distance that fosters growth? Can we really free others from our own needs for them so they can unfold their lives in NAMELESS' ways? Can we really allow others to be who they are? Can we let others become what they choose to become?
Can we — I — you — really be-for-others by being-apart-from-others?

In the necessity for c-o-n-n-e-c-t-i-o-n we forget that ultiMATE growth comes from **GOD**. We are means and never the end. We never know enough to decide for others what it means for them to live. We can stand by others,
yet we can never
stand in place of others.
In the end our efforts are always preliminary.
We prepare the way;

NAMELESS alone gives
life
love
light.

We move aPART from each other in a relatedness
that limits expansiveness   and   liberates humanness.[34]

A highway shall be there,
and it shall be called the Holy Way. . . .

Isaiah 35:8 (RSV)

''I am the Way. . . .''

John 14:6 (RSV)

. . . belonging to the Way. . . .

Acts 9:2 (RSV)

6

getting from here-to-there: beyond ambiguity

We all travel. From the very beginning people have been on the move. We are ever looking for something: food, shelter, and comfort; living space and elbow room; meaning and purpose.[35] Every question lays bare a quest. Whether we think of physical space or universal-personal pilgrimage, God's **QUEST**ion, ''Where are you?'' suggests an answer in the image of transportation.

We seek ways of getting from here-to-   there!

As we discussed earlier, all people are caught up in the quest for connection. We search for ways of

breaking-O U t of limited living,

making-way for what matters,

being-IN-TOUCH with each other,

lINking-up all creation.

We long to make and keep life truly human. We would make kNOWn the ✖ of genuine Community.

But by what means can we get from here-to-   there? What ways are available? All we know is the necessity for finding ways. If "the bomb" does not get us, our civiLIzEd progress will. For we are threatened by our productive capacity even more than by our destructive capability.

Mauldin © 1967 Chicago Sun-Times
'Thank heaven it was only pollution, not a nuclear bomb'

Lord of the Flies, by William Golding, dramatizes our predicament. A group of British boys are shipwrecked on an uninhabited island. They have no way of getting from the isolation of the island to the community on the mainland. They are cut-off.

Initially, they work to get rescued. Their child-leader, however, senses an insidious symptom:

> "Meetings. Don't we love meetings? Everyday. Twice a day. We talk. . . . I bet . . . this minute, they'd come running. Then we'd be, you know, very solemn and someone would say we ought to build a jet, or a submarine, or a TV set. When the meeting was over they'd work for five minutes, then wander   off or go hunting." [36]

The boys talked big yet did little.

As their life together falls apart, one boy declares, "We need an assembly. Not for fun. Not for laughing and falling off the log . . . not for making jokes, or for . . . cleverness. Not for these things. But to put things straight."

[36] Reprinted by permission of Coward-McCann, Inc.

More power does not mean better people.

Later, another wistfully observes, if only the adults could get a message to us. If only they could send us something

GROWN-UP

. . .

a sign

or something.

The short attention span and casual concern of the boys abort efforts to be rescued. Cooperation disintegrates. When someone mentions "rescue," the others try to remember what "rescue" means. At the end only savagery and terror reign.

That pessimistic picture of human (?) relatedness (??) underscores our situation. We <u>are</u> long on talk and short on follow through. Life <u>does</u> get muddled and then goes mad. We <u>do</u> need an assembling "to put things straight." Our meetings prevent our meeting.

But how can that be? According to the biblical understanding of life and loaf and love, all — biochemical, psycho-social, politico-economic, meaning-valuing — diMENsions were created basically good (Genesis 1:1–2:3). In getting from creative potential to fulfilled actual, the **ORDERING** LORd **GOD** decreed that persons be loved and things be used:

You shall love God
and
neighbor
as
yourself.

You shall have power over
every living
thing/
concept/
place/
experience.

But we reverse that proper **ORDERING** of **I AM**-therefore-you are. More often than not we U S e persons and love things.[37] Not beIng-in-tOUCH with personal **ME**aning, we overinvest in impersonal **MEAN**s. C/u.t#$o@f*f((from intimacy, caring, giving/receiving, we are locked into isolation, indifference, stagnation, and obsessive possession. We experience a chasm between our frustration with what is and the fullness of what might be. Commerce replaces community.

The world is God's, not ours. We cannot do with it as we please. When we reverse HIS ordering we inevitably are destroyed. That which goes against the grain of creation eventually collapses. God overthrows loving "out-of-order" — that is, whatever loves and is loved inordinately. His reordering activity mercifully destroys using persons and loving things. His reconciling activity justly reestablishes **loving** persons and **using** things.

How can we get a grasp of the meaning and means by which we can reorder persons and things? What kind of conceptual image can aid us in comprehending the human quest?

A clue comes from the place Palestine held in relation to the larger ancient world. From early times Palestine was the bridge, the highway, connecting the empires of the Nile Valley in Egypt with the fertile plains of Mesopotamia. Little Palestine served as <u>the</u> way for linking Africa and Asia. Hence, the disruption of roads warned of misfortune 33:7-9), while the construction of roads prophesied good fortune (Isaiah 40:3-5). In the time of fulfillment, lands and people would be linked by "a highway" (Isaiah 19:23-25) .

It should not surprise us, therefore, that in the arid, barren, empty richness of human potential the summons came

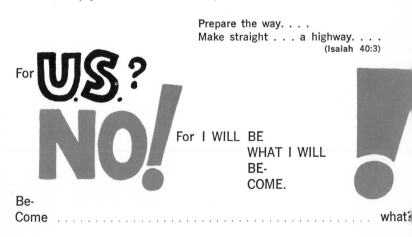

Prepare the way. . . .
Make straight . . . a highway. . . .
(Isaiah 40:3)

For **U.S.?**
NO! For I WILL BE
WHAT I WILL
BE-
COME.

Be-
Come . . . . what?

In Jesus-whom-we-call-the-Christ, we receive the sign of the grown-up, **ORDERING** us from the chaos of our here to the fulfillment of h**IS** t**HERE:**

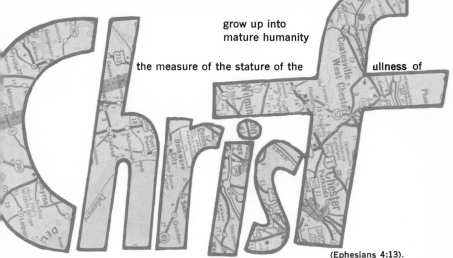

grow up into
mature humanity

the measure of the stature of the   ullness of

(Ephesians 4:13).

We are c**ALL**ed to BE-
COME . . . . mature persons by ordering
mature community.

The martyred German pastor-theologian, Dietrich Bonhoeffer, reminded us to avoid religious arrogance that insists that to be a man is to be a Christian. Instead he affirmed the religious reality that proclaims: to be Christian is to be man!

"To be a Christian

does not mean to be religious in a <u>particular</u> way, to cultivate some <u>particular</u> form of asceticism (as a sinner, a penitent or a saint), but

to be a man. It is

not some religious act which makes a Christian what he is, but

participation in the suffering of God in the life of the world." [38]

To belong to the ordered community that calls Christ its head is to put things straight (Hebrews 12:13)— that means, to be**LONG** to **THE WAY** that makes possible people becoming

human   mature   full-grown.

        The ordered community represents a new clarity regarding the meaning of hu**MAN**ity **IN COMMUNITY**. More than one hundred different words are used in the New Testament for the Church-as-ordered-community. The word "church" comes from the Greek word <u>ecclesia,</u> which implies an assembly of persons summoned for a particular purpose by God through Christ. These hundredfold expressions of <u>ecclesia</u> have been grouped into ten categories:

saints and sanctified
believers and faithful
slaves and servants
the people of God
kingdom and temple
household and family
the new exodus
vineyard and flock
one body in Christ
and

In New Humanity [39]
    people break through dividing walls
    of hostility. . . .
        people are for people . . .
      people hold together in love and by love

for nAMeless-✖︎ 's sake
and
in the power of
that which WILL CAUSE TO BE-
COME.

In Christ our quest for connecting you-and-me, meaning-and-power, is-
and-ought is fulfilled. **HE**re **IS** the **WAY.**
We belong to him.

What might it mean for the
Church to be/come the Way of New
Humanity? How do we prepare that Way?
How can we make straight genuine Com-
munity? How might we, in Spirit and in
Truth, become "nothing but a section of
humanity in which Christ has really taken
form"? [40]

Let your imagination play with
the idea of (Church?) Community as highway and byway.

What comes to mind? —

inner loops and outer loops
rivers of concrete
on-ramps for entrances
off-ramps for exits
signs for distances
s t r e t c h e s f o r s p e e d i n g
signs for directions
places for stopping

wormlike threads twisting in and around and around over and under

Our great highway system probably symbolizes "the only truly communal
architecture in the country today." [41] It
organizes, channels, connects, and directs
our separate yet interdependent living.
We all travel from private worlds of home

and intimacy to the public world of commerce and culture. Freeways flood morning and evening with the ebb and flow into and out from the giant octopus. Thruways strain with incessant pounding from place to place to place to place to place.

Those means by which we get around are impersonal and innocent. They are available to anyone for any purpose. The meaning of those means, however, depends upon the commitment of the people using them.

As means, a Way (1) enables us to break-out of the boxes in which we are trapped and (2) provides an instrument that makes-way for our intentions.

As meaning, a Way discloses our (1) being-in-touch with persons, and (2) being linked with reality.

Because we live in community we are tied in with both private worlds and public world. The transition from one to the other can be jolting and disruptive and upending.

IN THE PRIVATE WORLD OF HOME AND INTIMACY, *attention cherishes the person speaking, the leisure waiting, the letting-go, in short, the freedom to be. Here we know the personal structures of sociability and friendship, of neighborhood and group, of family and care, of tenderness and affection. The time to relate and the possibility of closeness wrap us in a mantle of warmth. We are renewed as persons because we relate as persons.*

In the public world of commerce and culture, energy concentrates on the job to be done, the lessons to be learned, the schedule to be met, in short, on the demand to do. Here we experience the impersonal structures of school and business, of industry and finance, of entertainment and government. The pressure for accomplishment and the demand for achievement over-ride all else. The necessary act takes precedence over the acting person.

Today the public world grows larger while the private world grows smaller . The impersonal necessity of doing is segregated from the personal freedom to be. Only by combining freedom to do the necessary act with the necessity of being the acting person do we begin to reorder the world in God's way. For then we reestablish our rightful rule over everything and our loving relationship with every person.

The Way frees us to take part in <u>the structures of community</u> (the parts of life) <u>as means</u> and to be part of <u>the community of structures</u> (the pattern of life) <u>as meaning</u>. Or, to put the matter in terms of decisions involved in transportation development:

> "No longer is it sufficient for a highway to carry vehicles efficiently and speedily from Point A to Point B. Now, it is felt, a highway should melt esthetically into a neighborhood. It should contribute to development of the neighborhood's economic and social life. It should disrupt and uproot minimally." [42]

I have picked up the image of (Church) Community as highway for two reasons:

deeply embedded in Scripture we find the orienting-image of (Church) Community as highway. The highway symbol gives focus and form to God's reconciling activity.

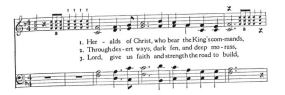

Community (Way) as the meaning — the intention — of life: religious symbols usually elicit primarily the deeply personal experiences — the private world of the individual. Yet we live in a time when the private is dominated by the public, when the impersonal rules the personal. To minister to our time we need an orienting image that catches up the sense of Community as means as well as meaning. Therefore,

The symbol of highway opens up the meaning of divine in**TENT**ion:

1. Her - alds of Christ, who bear the King's com-mands,
2. Through des - ert ways, dark fen, and deep mo - rass,
3. Lord, give us faith and strength the road to build,

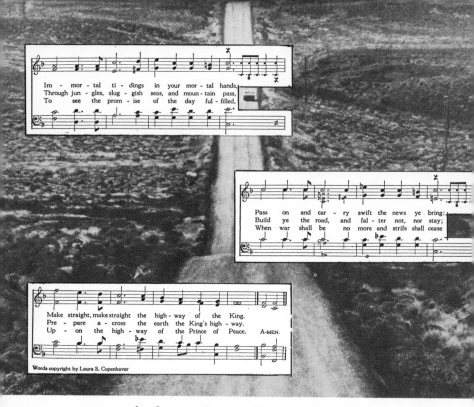

Im - mor - tal ti - dings in your mor - tal hands,
Through jun - gles, slug - gish seas, and moun - tain pass,
To see the prom - ise of the day ful - filled,

Pass on and car - ry swift the news ye bring;
Build ye the road, and fal - ter not, nor stay;
When war shall be no more and strife shall cease

Make straight, make straight the high - way of the King.
Pre - pare a - cross the earth the King's high - way.
Up - on the high - way of the Prince of Peace. A-MEN.

Words copyright by Laura S. Copenhaver

As Community, the Church only points toward and prepares the way for New Creation. The church itself is never fulfilled Community. The communities of this world are to be- come the Community of our Lord and of his Christ (Revelation 11:15).

Nevertheless, the task of preparation — of being highway — is sobering. As one contemporary prophet declares:

"If there is any weakness in the Church's preaching, it lies in sentimentally putting forth the Gospel without preparing the way." [43]

Thus we face the questions:

How can the church be the Way for genuine Community?
How can the church be the way of genuine Community?

It is to these questions of the means of highway and the meaning of highway that we turn the rest of our attention.

"See, I am making all things new. . . ."

Revelation 21:5 (Phillips)

If any one is in Christ, he is a new creation;
the old has passed away, behold, the new has come. . . .

2 Corinthians 5:17 (RSV)

. . . it does not yet appear what we shall be,
but we know . . . we shall be like him. . . .

1 John 3:2 (RSV)

7

celebrating: breaking-out in possibility

SING A NEW SONG (Psalm 96:1)!
A new day has dawned!
A new order is here (2 Corinthians 5:17)!
A new relationship has appeared (1 Corinthians 11:23-26)!

There is no-thing new under the sun. Where is anything of which it can be said, "See, this is new"? (Ecclesiastes 1:2-10)? Look around. All you can see is an end-less pounding of samenesssamenesssameness sameness. We are as tRAPPED as we ever were. Egypt is everywhere. Roads only lead to dead ends.

person

same purposes
same crosses
same curses
same ideals
same ideas

No! Something _has_ happened! An unexpected opening looms before us. The possibility of becoming like Him — the indwelling _Christ_ — t**HE** new **REAL**ity — the new city — _one_ heaven — _one_ earth — _one_ people — genuine comm**U-NITY** — is here and now in our midst.

A Way has been prepared. A Way has been set forth. A Way is available. We are on the Way because a roadway is at hand. Having broken-out in faith, we can now venture with trust.

But you will rightly ask: What is the Way like? Of what does the New Order consist? What may we expect?

I cannot tell in advance. Nobody can know ahead of time. We only know it will be startlingly unexpected (Isaiah 48:6-8).

An old Jewish legend tells that when Moses stood at the edge of the Red Sea the waters did not divide. Only after the first man risked all by _jumping_ — only then did the waters divide — only then could the people-in-relationship pass through safely.[44]

We have to _jump_ to know. We have to die to live. We have to let go to find out.

The prepared Way is like any trip. We only know in general where we are going. We have maps. The car is in condition. The time to leave is set . . . and we start. . . .

ment excitement excitement excitement excitement excitement exc

That is the fIrst and crucial f**ACT** of the roadWay. We engage the transmission, press the accelerator and drive off. Instead of endless committee meetings committee meetings meetingmeetingmeeting — we simply let go of endless endless possibilities

for the sake of concrete actualities.

The letting go may make us a bit dizzy, but the roadWay pulsates with excitement. It bubbles with youth's in-sistence:

"Put the show on the road!"

"Let's get going."

"Forget the past. Today's what counts!"

This is the day the Lord has made!

This is the day the Lord has made!

This is the day the Lord has made!

This is the day the Lord has made!

(Psalm 118:24)

The time is always here (John 7:6b).

The genuine is at hand.

Turn around — give yourself to

I AM BE-COMING ALL IN ALL (Mark 1:15)

Today — today — today — today — today

too (Acts 17:6) Or is it,

here — here — here — here — here — here — here — here — here — here

those who upset the world have come

those who right the world have come HERE — THANK GOD! Not the same old things in the new old ways, but some new thing because of new reality.

In strange lands (and today our land is strange) and strange times (and today our times are strange), the old songs no longer stir us, cut adrift as we are from the source of their inspiration (Psalm 137:1-4). If, however, one is in Christ, he is new **BEING**; the old has passed away, the now of possi-bility has coME.

Without excitement we die. No place beckons. No person calls. No purpose pulls. We remain bound up in our bantam worlds, feeding upon ourselves, seeing only ourselves, bored with only ourselves. Everything has been tried; every idea expressed; every possibility explored.

"WE HAVE ALWAYS DONE IT THIS WAY"

"THERE'S NO USE IN TRYING — NOBODY CARES."

"WE TRIED THAT AND IT DIDN'T WORK."

Do not look back.
Do not go back.

Look ahead.
Move on (Luke 9:57-62).

Respond
even though it changes you!

At their best, young people pursue the excitement lying in wait on the road. They press the immediacy of life, the intensity of experience, the necessity of doing. They spur us on to plunge into concrete and common experience for in-spired living.

"When do facts become interesting?
When do words recover their meaning?

When they again appear
as things to come,
as acts to be done,
as names to be invoked. . . ." [45]

"I am waiting
for a rebirth of wonder. . . ." [46]

"A rebirth of wonder" bursts forth as the power of a second wind in a hard race, as the spark of a new intimacy in a moment of meeting, as the "I SEE!" of the discovery of a new connectedness. We give ourselves to what is taking place. It matters, so we are preSENT — tHERE — with it, which is what love is!

But the excitement of be
coming anything and every
after novelty (Acts 17:21). The
can be someBODY — the liv
tion — not just any society
THE roaDwAY requires the e
best, it likewise demands
at its best.
A trip implies destina
therefore decision. What do
Do we turn this way or that?
do we rest?

coming does not mean be-
thing. We too easily chase
good news emphasizes we
ing organism of God's crea-
but genuine commUNITY. If
xcitement of youth at its
the perSpEctivE of adulthood

tion — direction — and
we take? What do we leave?
How far shall we go? When

empHasIS emphasIs emphasIs emphasIS emphasIS emphasIs

Adult perspective asks
what is possible?
feasible?
desirable?
unavoidable?
appropriate?
"The time is now!!!!!!"

For youth the demand is:
For adults the issue is: "Which
time is now —

waiting?	acting?
responding?	resting?
planting?	plucking?
breaking down?	building up?
weeping?	laughing?
embracing?	confronting?
seeking?	losing?"

(Ecclesiastes 3:1-8).

Times differ. Perspective en tails knowing what
time it is, what action is called for, what action is rejected.

We face the necessity of sac rifice. We must decide
to take different roads for dif ferent purposes at different times. Moments of mean ing are "pregnant moments" — moments in which so mething comes alive —
moments of birth and rebirth (whether of a people,
a group, a person, or an affec tion).

Perspective also includes in sight. Insight is seeing into what is going on. It is the discovery of what
makes something "tick." Our eyes open. We come alive.
We know who we are. We see what is what. We realize
what must be done.

While dawn is breaking, we still travel a long
night's journey into day. But t he grown-up EMPHASIS
— what kind of action at this time in this place —
heralds I AM BREAKING-OUT IN POSSIBILITY.
As members of Christ's body we not only recognize
moments of meaning, we also pro claim one moment of
meaning, one right time, one cl arifying event —

the time is fulfilled
the secret is out
the mystery is known
(Ephesians 3:3-6).

In Christ we discover the meaning of all moments. Just as Greenwich is the standard by which we regulate clocks, so Christ is the standard by which we check timing and meaning. Just as it is important to know "what makes us tick," so it is important to know "what time to keep."

As those who are growing up in Christ, we see the answer to what time to keep. In Jesus-as-the-Christ God has made known his purpose and has made clear his understanding of humanity. In Jesus Christ we see the **INNER ME**aning of time, namely

— the bringing together of that which has been torn apart within persons and among groups.
— the conquering of hostility by seeing through it to the inner hurt of being unrecognized and cut-off
— the acknowledging of our need for meaning as well as others' need for meaning
(Ephesians 2:11-22).

Grown-up emphasis matches youth's excitement. That we are to be "on the road" is unquestioned. Which road to be on at which time is always the question. Emphasis — perspective — sacrifice is a matter of experience. We examine what happens. We reflect on intentions. We analyze unanticipated consequences. We evolve a body of understood wisdom.

Without such living memory we never grow up. Like Peter Pan, we remain eternally kids, little children in adult bodies. Like children we then flit from fad to fad. Each emotion bears the same intensity. Every thought carries the same weight. There is no differentiation.

When we grow up, we put away childish ways (1 Corinthians 13:11). We sense what we are about. We see what is to be done. We act in appropriate ways.

In the Old Testament the people freed from bondage found themselves among people tied to nature. Springsummer fallwinterspringsummerfallwinter. Natural powers; nature gods. Cyclical rhythm goes on and on and on by going round and round and round. It never gets anywhere. Worshipers of the status quo experience only the limits of what has been — cultivate soil, fertilize womb and flock, produce long life and well-being. Celebrators of breaking-out, however, discern limitless possibilities —

create society

call men

humanize humanity.

The emphasis of clarified experience baptizes the excitement of passionate longing. What gives life is met in history, not in nature — in exodus and easter, in liberation and life, in **THE** de**MAN**d to decide what matters, in persisting faithfully and **ACT**ing responsibly.

Because of what has happened, the world lies open. The issue is not the tradition of the past but the tradition of the promise. What matters is the right ordering of genuine reality. The presence of the community of faith with a communion table at its center testifies to living sacrifice. We keep the wounds of life be**FOR**e **US**. We are reminded of what we are about.

Life now stands forth as crucial, decisive, demanding; this face; this place; this conflict; this sacrifice.

We move from right faith to true hope by concrete acts of love here and now. We move from right emphasis to true openness by specific acts of limitation here and now.

We learn what to exalt and what to ignore. We admit a breakdown in connection between the generations. Unless we die (Romans 6:1-11; Philippians 3:10) . . . .

Even though the decisive moment of meaning has come, the time of fulfillment is still coming. That is why we speak of the second coming of ✗ at the end of time. The ripening of humanity is now understood. The process is underWay. But the fullness — in which God is all in all, in which hurts are healed and the lion lies down with the lamb — only appears at the end of history (Isaiah 65:17-25; Revelation 21:1-4; 2 Peter 3:10-13).

The breaking through of Humanity ever and always goes before us. God was ahead of us in our escape from being boxed-in (Deuteronomy 31:7-8). God goes before us in our search for the recovery of life (Mark 16:7). God is never in the past but ever in the future; never among the lifeless (Luke 24:5) but only among the living (Matthew 28:20); never in the incompleteness of the present but always in the power of that which is still to come (Hebrews 6:5)!

The knowledge of openness — time fulfilled only at the end of time — calls into question everything that is in service to that which is to come. We worship God, not his creation. He sets before us an open highWay — many possibilties, many routes, many directions, many demands, many decisions. Not every road is

85

"TO EXIST
for the future of others
without being suffocated
by their present." [47]

desirable. Not every road is good. Yet we move into the unpredictable because **HE WILL BE HE**re. Every road is usable. Every road carries us on the Way. No road finally gets in the way (Romans 8:28).

Process —
movement is the
ing on the Way.
of creating — re-
newing — innovating.
has its own task. No
the only task.

change — turmoil —
experience of be-
We take the risk
viewing — re-
Each time
time has

In the event of Jesus the Christ a dynamic future broke into a static present. In that event a decisive advance of the whole against the part took place. "Salvation came into a world of many gods, many lands, many peoples. Over against each of these it sets up a singular: one God, one world, one humankind." [48] And precisely because of that singleness of God/world/ humanity, the richness of diversity lies before us.

The promise of the King's highWay has opened three successive routes from a fragmented present into a unifying future: [49]

ONE GOD	ONE WORLD
A.D.	1000
saints and martyrs <u>withdrew from</u> this world of competing gods to be the Body of a **GENUINE UNIVERSE.**	pilgrims and crusaders and missionaries <u>traveled through</u> this world of "unconnected countries and undiscovered lands" to loosen local ties by forming a **GENUINE EARTH.**

ONE HUMANKIND

2000

laity and secularist
<u>move into</u>
society
to reunite the
broken family of man
and to reinspire
the ways by which
people make it in
the world via a
birth of **GENUINE
RELATEDNESS.**

Hope works within every period, every place, every people, every person in astonishing ways. People-of-the-road-Way respect precedent (Matthew 5:17-20), yet live freely. There are many expressways into New City (Revelation 21:12, 25). There are many rooms in the New Home (John 14:2). There is nothing — helpful nor harmful, desirable nor undesirable, present nor possible — that can stop the movement of meaning in mankind (Romans 8:35-39). The roadWay flows with traffic. Even

de
to
ur
s

and disasters <u>can</u> perform useful functions — for those who carry within themselves the opening **WORLD** of hope (Romans 8:28). The promise is coming true: I <u>will</u> <u>be</u> with you even until the end of time (Matthew 28:20)! And in that promise we are "given the prospect of a new ability to be."[50]

Now you are the body of Christ. . . .
      1 Corinthians 12:27 (RSV)

8
nurturing: genuinely making-way

DIRECTION

"Living faith means growing form." [51]

EXPERIENCE

"Since I joined the church," one church member said, "I have given most of my free time to it and, frankly, I have not grown in my Christian life at all. I am so bogged down in the mechanics, the busy work of attending meetings, of dealing with methods and mastering procedures that I am missing what it is all about."

CONCLUSION

"The churchification of the world
is [not] its salvation. . . ." [52]

The means by which we get things done often cancel the purpose for which we are using them. Methods have a way of negating goals. Organization tends to get-in-the-way.

Yet we cannot escape organization. Even such a simple (□?□!□) relationship as the family requires it. The issue is not whether we organize but rather how we organize. How can the means we use accomplish the meanings we intend?

Recently, a powerful but silent revolution has taken place. Television has replaced the radio as the major medium in the home. That shift illustrates the revolution. Our attention turns from hearing to seeing, from the ear to the eye.[53] Actions replace words. The communication of possibility demands live demonstration more than mere description, real results more than careful definition.

How can we live with one another?
How can life be set straight?
How can community be genuine?
How can we disclose the King's highWay?

If separated people and separated places are to be joined to the whole created world, four processes appear basic (Acts 2:41-47). Without such processes it is doubtful whether churches show forth Christ's Way. Those necessary and sufficient means for genuine meaning are celebrating, appropriating, deepening, and confirming.

Celebrating breaking bre and prayin

Without knowing what to emphasize and what to ignore, chaos reigns.

Special events, red letter days, birthdays, anniversaries and holidays all call attention to who we are. They highlight what has happened to us. These events lift up the meanings of our lives. Without them everything blends into endless sameness, rushing emptiness, frantic searching, and desperate cautiousness. Because of them everything takes on freshness and vitality. They bring constant recovery.

Birthdays provide an analogy for the meaning of celebration. A definite, unchangeable day on the calendar fixes the appearance of every individual. Each year, family and friends are reminded of that fact. "The universe resounds with the joyful cry I am." [54] Candles on the cake evidence the unfolding years. We celebrate this person's presence!

Similarly, Pentecost marks the birthday of Community. When people understood each other, community appeared. Thus, Sunday is party-time. We identify those who are here because of Christ's death-resurrection event. We solemnize the healing of the hurt of the world by remembering the wound of the Word —

> without the shedding of blood
> there is no remission of sin
> (Hebrews 9:22)

> this is my body which is broken for you;
> this is my blood which is spilled for you;
> as often as you celebrate my presence,
> you make known the meaning of what matters.
> (1 Corinthians 11:23-26)

An act of celebration provides an ongoing structure which reminds us of the wound. It lifts up sorrow and joy, tragedy and triumph, the routine and the unusual in ritual form. As celebrators, we recall what has happened to us and for us — the mighty events of meaning (Psalm 105:1-42). We rehearse what we are to do — the meaningful act (Psalm 105: 43-45).

Because we bind present experience together with previous experience, we can move more freely into unfolding and uncertain experience. Scattered chords are disciplined into an orderly symphony — a hymn to joy!

> We are here for making man;
> Man is here in Jesus Christ!

> Celebrate the humanity of God;
> Humanize the humanity of man!

By our celebration we answer the question:

WHY DO WE BOTHER?

APPROPRIATING

learning teachings of the apostles 2

Without faithful understanding, celebration easily degenerates into an emotional binge or an empty ritual. With faithful understanding, celebration makes the means of meaning genuine. Then celebration serves man and not man celebration (Mark 2:27-28) .

Understanding connects disjointed experiences. It brings together various aspects of life in a way that "makes sense" of what happens. Such appropriating embraces all those ideas, values, and thoughts that deal explicitly with the significance of experience. The content focuses directly upon those realities that matter to people as people.

As Christ's Body, we have received a particular way of thinking and working and living. The **exodus** — *EASTER* drama discloses the ways men hurt and the hope that heals. The ultimate power working in life restores rather than destroys humanness. The ultimate meaning working in the world is purposeful rather than purposeless. In-spiriting comes from the wedding of power and meaning.

In contrast, fanciful understanding makes no reference to the beyond in the midst of the here. People consequently lack shared experience. We are then without common memory or common hope. We can refer neither to the source of our beginning nor to the calling forth of our becoming. The focus is strictly this-worldly.

Genuine understanding instructs people in question-asking and question-answering: IN THE LIGHT OF WHAT GOD HAS DONE, WHAT IS HE NOW DOING? Every fresh form appears when living faith leads us to ask:

— what is the truth of this situation?
— what do we intend to do/what are we seen as doing?
— what does our style of responding "say" about what matters?
— what does it mean to be responsible here and now?

Appropriating must occur in a context. That con-**TEXT** may be

person   place   problem   predicament

but, regardless of the particular, appropriating unites the ever-lasting with the everyday.

Specific experiences and general understanding are shared. Ideas flow back-and-forth between youngest/oldest, between the most marginal/the most central, between members/minister, between world/church. There comes a continuous giv-ing-and-taking of suggestions, of criticisms, of helpful encour-agement, of recognition and of confirmation.

By appropriating we answer the question:

WHAT CAN THIS EXPERIENCE MEAN?

Deepening

joining in fellowship

The deepening process
influences the ways members
of the community get along. It catches up what the community does and how it does it.

Genuine deepening means moving BEneath the surface to expose what is there. Indirectly <u>and</u> directly questions are raised that sharpen the personal meanings of a situation:

— who are <u>you</u>?
       — what matters to <u>you</u>?
       — with what do <u>you</u> struggle?
— what do <u>you</u> want?

From such give-and-take, personal response is de-manded. Disruption may take place. Concern can easily boil into conflict. But, in the process,

PEOPLE will be open with each other,
PEOPLE will be taking responsibility,
PEOPLE will be reconciling differences.
Genuine means restore the courage to know others and the courage to be known by others.[55]

In contrast, false means keep relationships restricted to the superficial. Any questioning or probing or deeper **ME**aning is indirect at best or a**VOIDED** at worst. We experience no demand for personal confrontation or personal encounter. Differences are minimized. Similarities are exaggerated. We tiptoe around everything touchy. The impersonal and the conventional are emphasized. We transfer responsibility from ourselves to others. What happens is up to them. We have no part in it.

In genuine deepening, mutuality, reciprocity and caring tend to predominate. Defensiveness and deception wane. ThEre iS No STeReotYPed waY OF InteraCTinG. Instead there is

Surprise

the spontaneous

the unexpected

Whatever comes, we cannot not respond.

To shun growing pains contributes to childish retardation. To avoid stress arrests development. To ward off contact spawns sterility. Without the stress of growing pains we lose our ability to produce and to reproduce.

Christian culture has mistakenly conveyed the notion that to be upset and to upset are sin. We are supposed to encourage sweetness and light. Christians then find themselves in a bind because they tend to see the meaning of reconciliation without understanding the means by which reconciliation comes.

Deepened contact between people depends upon an atmosphere of risk-and-trust. We risk being knowing; we trust openness. Nothing necessary to the relationship can be withheld. Everything crucial to the relationship must be handled. To receive one another by allowing differences requires that we structure less and be surprised more. We give up mOLDing others into our own IMAGE. Being certain who we are, we can encourage others to be who they are.

As a result, we no longer fear looking at each other's hopes and hurts. In fact, not to look is to die; to look is to live (Numbers 21:4-9).

Put on the new nature
created after the likeness of
I AM WHAT I AM BECOMING.

therefore putting away falsehood
let every one speak the truth
with his neighbor
in love
(Ephesians 4:15, 24-26)

Each of us comes at the world with unique equipment. We see differently; we organize differently; we evaluate differently. No two people encounter the same situation in exactly the same way. We are, in truth, individuals in our biological equipment, in our social conditioning, and in our integrating of the two. Instead of wondering at the wide variation of reactions among people, we ought to wonder when there is no variation. By ignoring individuality we miss individuals. By deepening we answer the question: WHO ARE WE?

Confirmin

Celebrating,
appropriating, and
deepening
flow into confirming

Sharing- everything in common

any one is
boxed-in
in-the-way
out-of-touch
cut-off

Then we
are also !

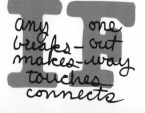
any one
breaks-out
makes-way
touches
connects

then!
we do also

If

we bother
understand
relate

then

we let others know

TRUE

REALITY

HUMANITY

COMMUNITY

If there is no life together, there is no life. Life together aids meaning because such interdependency constitutes the meaning of meaning. To hang on to what matters as a private possession is to lose what matters. To let be/come what matters as a shared reality that grounds and calls forth everyone is to find what matters (Isaiah 58:6-12).

Means which are genuine let others know of New Humanity and enable people to participate in New Community. They enable us to give and receive, to serve and be served, to turn outward and inward, to seek the neighbor-in-the-stranger and the stranger-in-the-neighbor. We know the means we use are genuine to the extent they take the form of Christ in the world. That form opens a usable future for the limited, liberates those who are imprisoned, restores sight to the blinded, frees those who are constricted and makes known acceptance of being (Luke 4:16-21).

As the highWay of Christ, we face two tasks:

1 establishing and maintaining connections for getting to different places for different purposes

2 developing and cultivating those different places for their different purposes

Match each setting below with a corresponding experience. You might draw connecting lines. You might write each setting and each experience on separate pieces of paper. **2** Which experiences enable you to cultivate the purpose of a particular setting? **1** Which experiences enable you to connect one setting with (an)other setting(s)?

Try various combinations. See what happens to the way you feel about the world. For example, if school expresses learning, can business? If home expresses intimacy, can culture? Is life so compartmentalized and encapsulated that unsuspecting possibilities are unavailable in our various "worlds"?

SETTING		EXPERIENCE	
1.	school	a.	learning
2.	home	b.	intimacy
3.	commerce	c.	servicing
4.	business	d.	industry
5.	recreation	e.	playfulness
6.	culture	f.	seriousness
7.	church	g.	beyondness

If living faith means growing form, then there is no set or sure way of making known New Humanity in genuine Community. We engage in continuous clarification ➔ action/ action ➔ clarification/clarification ➔ action. We ask of every situation:

What is going on? What is taking place?
What helps the process? What gets in the way?

Such reflective-questioning communicates that meetings are for meeting, programming is process, means are for meaning. Genuine letting-be allows what is the truth to be present and trusted. When **1** connecting and **2** cultivating take place, then the means of this world have become the meaning of Humanity. When we serve, we answer the question:

WHAT DO WE DO?

. . . you who once were far off have been brought
near in the life blood of Christ . . . who has made
us both one, and has broken down the dividing wall
of hostility. . . .

Ephesians 2:13-14

Where two . . . are gathered in my name,
there am I. . . .

Matthew 18:20 (RSV)

9

sharing:
touching persons

. . . That's what's needed, don't you see?
<u>That!</u>
Nothing else matters half so much. To re-
assure one another. To answer each other. Perhaps
only <u>you</u> can listen to me and not laugh. Everyone
has, inside himself . . . what shall I call it?

A piece of **GOOD NEWS!**

Everyone is . . .
    a very great,
      very important
        character! . . .

Everyman must be persuaded — even if he's in
rags — that
      he's
      immensely,
      immensely,
      important! [56]

The means of community include main roads, side roads, connecting arteries. Without people traveling from place to place, however, these roads and arteries are **MEANingLESS**. They would simply stand empty and useless. They exist to be used — to take people places that matter to them. Similarly, the highWay is prepared for the recovery of humanity. Without people — you — I — others — going from place to place for purposes that make a difference, there can be no **MeANing**.

Yet it is not enough for us to be in specific places all by ourselves. We are born, we grow, we become, we are affirmed, we are confirmed only by our receiving-giving/giving-receiving to/from one another as real people (Matthew 25:31-46). The in-spiriting I Am Becoming requires us to recover each other's personhood. We are communicators of Christ to the degree we are communers in ChrISt. We show forth the good news of the possibility of inexhaustible humanizing by living ourselves into-the-world as persons. Deeper than ideas we throw around is the contact we establish with each other — Pentecost, if you will, NEW HUMANITY in NEW CITY.

To recover persons is no easy task. The melancholy Søren Kierkegaard warned against too close contact. ". . . it is impossible," he claimed, "for one human being to be anything to another human being except to be in his way." Later, however, in that same volume he made an additional observation: "He who cannot reveal himself cannot love, and he who cannot love is the most unhappy man of all." [57]

Kierkegaard reminds us of the impossibility of not getting in each other's way. Equally he reminds us of the necessity of giving ourselves to one another. The surest Way to transform alienation into reconciliation is to let others know who we are and what we experience. [58]

Self-disclosure as a means for recovering persons implies a recovery of trust. One individual described the experience to me this way:

> My experience seems to show me a pattern in all my relationships. There seems to be an initial resistance — when I ask myself if I really want to become involved, vulnerable, and possibly suffer hurt and rejection.

k risk risk risk risk risk risk risk risk

Then there seems to be a battle in which we are each trying to establish our position in relation to the other. There are ups and downs of emotion, perhaps quarrels and many doubts.

After this comes a period of tentative acceptance and growing agreement; as the relationship matures there comes the feeling of nonpossessing love, which has a steadfastness and a sustaining quality that brings peace, fulfillment, and vitality.

Frankly, the early stages of trusting are filled with risk. To trust means I have to let you (or someone like you) know — really kn**OW** — what I am experiencing. I have to let you see the me behind the mask.

But, and here is the risk, if you see the me behind the mask, you may rebuff me or **RID**icul**E** me or reject me. If I let you see my need, you have "the power to harm easily." [59]

In the embryonic stage of humanizing, the margin of trust is small. Every response feels as though one's whole life is on the line. We experience ourselves as being potentially at the mercy of others.

At this **FOUND**ational l**EVE**l we ache to be recognized as persons. To let you know my **TENDER** inside is to put my life in your hands. I need to be affirmed as a human being. I want to be confirmed as someone who counts. To experience trust is to k**NOW** your supporting presence. It is to see in your eyes that i exist. The looks we receive from each other convey life or death, acceptance or rejection, even though no words may be spoken.

The look of seeing or not-seeing determines whether trust is recovered. The fate of nations as well as individuals depends upon such in-the-midst-of-you contact. Without recovering persons, the ordering structures of Christ are for naught. We r**Eco**VER tr**US**t to the degree we really see and confirm each other as human beings.

risk risk risk risk risk risk risk risk trust · risk · trust · risk · trust · risk · trust – risk-trust – risk-trust – risk-trust – risk – tru

Once trust takes root, the presence of humanness spreads. The cultivation of the personal follows. We reach out to others in tentatively little ways. Our cIrcle of cont**ACT** widens. Other people stop being "enemy" and become quite simply "other." One's view of the world changes:

> I'm not walking around afraid of everyone stepping on me any more. I can begin to listen to what they are saying. It's amazing but I'm not living with expectations any more. I always used to be thinking of what was going to happen and what could happen — only now it doesn't matter. All that matters is just living now. I figure I will be able to take care of what comes when it comes.

More deeply, a sense of responsibility takes root. We discover that we — you, I, everyone — possess the ability to respond to . . . well, another person put it to me this way:

> I couldn't understand it, but there came a strange sense of a greater feeling of responsibility, responsibility for the relationship with you and others also. . . . In the past I've had a shallow sense of responsibility. I always took responsibility and things like that, but the kind of responsibility I felt in my relationship with people was more like taking my turn in cleaning the house or visiting my family or things like that.

> But the strange new kind of responsibility is something deeper than that. It is more like "I matter in this relationship with you. I have some influence in your life as a person. While I do not mean nearly as much to you as I do to my friends and my family, I mean something!"

> It is a new and strange kind of responsibility that is unlike anything I have ever felt before.

> I matter! I mean something!

personal responsibility *personal* respor

When I experience myself as mattering, the personal dimension reemerges. If I mean something, then you mean something. And if you-and-I mean something together, that in-betweenness sparks the awareness of the indwelling Spirit — for wHERE as few as three or EVEn two are, tHERE is ChrISt in the WORLD.

That recovery of the personal enlarges with our being able to express what we experience. We put into words what we know inside. We let others know who we are by letting them know what we think and feel and fear and care about and hope for.

I cannot be certain what you experience unless you tell me clEARly. You, in turn, cannot be certain what I experience unless I tell you clEARLY. When we actually put into words what we are about, we humanize the prepared highWay. We communicate "the courage to be known."

Communicate Communicate Commun

Unfortunately, even when we want to humanize the highWay, we are never quite able to put into words all that we feel. Words have a way of meaning more than we intend. Words have a way of saying less than we desire. No word is so powerful that its meaning is unambiguously clear.

An ancient anecdote, probably of Indian origin, illustrates the way we depend upon shared experience and the interlocking meaning of words to convey what we want to tell the other: [60]

A blind man asked someone to explain the meaning of "white." "White is a color," he was told, "as for example white snow."

"I understand," said the blind man, "it is a cold and damp color."

"No, it doesn't have to be cold and damp. Forget about snow. Paper, for instance, is white."

"So it rustles?" asked the blind man.

"No indeed, it need not rustle. It is like the fur of an albino rabbit."

ity personal

"A soft, fluffy color?" the blind man wanted to know.

"It need not be soft either. Porcelain is white too."

"Perhaps it is a brittle color, then?" asked the blind man.

Since words only point toward experience and are never the experience itself, the power of a word to speak may be lost. What once bound us together may drive us apart. What once moved us may leave us unmoved. What once was a powerful word may have its day and be cancelled.

icate Communicate Com

Think of some of the great words that are losing their power to express experience. Such words would include love, joy, peace, meaningful. Traditional religious words, especially, have **LOST** the in-spiriting spARK. Words like sin, salvation, justification; even words like grace, Christ, Christian, God. These great dynamic words are half-dead, and for many are already buried.

In a way we can be grateful. Their death reminds us of what we so easily forget, namely, a map is not the territory.

SHISH KEBOB MARINADE

1 clove garlic, crushed	2 tbsp. dry mustard
1 c. cooking oil	1 tsp. salt
½ c. vinegar	¼ tsp. pepper
2 tsp. Worcestershire sauce	¼ tsp. ginger

is not

Words are not reality. Simply mouthing religious words is not the same as proclaiming good news.

Expression grows out of experience and in turn points back toward experience. When we lack shared experience, our words are impotent. Only by becoming aware of common experience will we recover the personal. Then communication will lead to communion.

But somehow even putting experience into words is never enough. The meaning of words depends upon our meeting as persons. Because we live in different worlds, we need direct contact. Communication takes place only when there is "a meeting of meaning between two or more persons." [61]

Contact enables us to say more of what we mean. It enables us to see more of what the other experiences. Behind casualness and conventionality we touch our inner selves.[62] Out of the give-and-take comes an increasing clarity of the meaning of words and, therefore, a fuller sharing in the experiences to which they refer. Someone has suggested a formula determining when we are free to speak:

> *I can only speak up for myself after I have restated the ideas and feelings of the previous speaker to that speaker's satisfaction.*[63]

icate Communicate

Just as I receipt a bill of goods, letting a store know that I have received what it intended in the condition it intended, so I let the other know I got what he intended to say. I hEAR him as he wants to be heard.

The give-and-take clarifies live expression of shared experience. The more fully we relate to each other, the more adequate the expression of our experience. The more adequate the expression of our experience, the more fully we relate to each other.

Part of the controversy in the New Testament church swirled around the interaction of the meaning-of-words and meeting-as-persons.

> Some insisted God had sent only words — the law and commandments. He had not come in person in the person of Jesus Christ.

> > Others insisted that in Jesus Christ we not only have words of God, but we also have Nameless Himself — Immanuel, God-with-us, personally, decisively, fully.

Today for many the Bible remains only a book of words. They experience no meeting with Jesus-the-Christ as Person. The living **Word** loses its power to speak because he is known only in verbal **FORM**.

To compound misunderstanding even more, much of our Protestant heritage has turned from an emphasis upon seeing to an emphasis upon hearing, from a religion of the to a religion of the  , from look-ing <u>at</u> an **eve**nt to h**EAR**ing <u>about</u> an event. Without intending it, much of Protestantism's emphasis upon the Word has tended to reproduce an increasing in**TELL**ectualization of real**IT**y. As a consequence, life has become sterilized.

The Tower of Babel reminds us we are out-of-touch. How can we transform words into WORD? How can we give up babbling on and on and on and on and speak a few words that say much? How does communication deepen into communion?

Since the Reformation, the Christian movement has been said to be carried wherever the Word was rightly preached and the sacraments properly administered. Today, however, God is focusing on active, participating laity.[64] People refuse to be bound any longer by decisions in which they do not take part. In and out of the church (community), people protest, strike, demand to be regarded as <u>human</u> participants. A new mark of the faithful community is emerging. It is seen wherever we come upon

open-faced discussion
conversation
talk that "levels"
d**I**alog**U**e.

For meaning to be real, the church (community) <u>must</u> link words and people. No longer can we hurl the good news into an unknown, hostile, or indifferent world. People come alive by touching each other as persons.

Straightforward conversation points toward a new style of ministry. Where people can talk together **I**n his n**AM**e, life is **PRESENT** (Matthew 18:20) . Where people congregate in the power of a caring concern that stands under each person's search for meaning, there is

REALITY IN THEIR MIDST:

> physical presence
> plus
> personal sharing,

a condition that does not guarantee living Word but one that prepares the Way.

Spirit is given **IN** the **MomENt** each of us understands his neighbor, even though we use different words and speak different languages. Then we know face-to-face. Just as we cannot be human alone, so we cannot find meaning alone.

As we can talk to each other
without too much self-
consciousness,
as we can speak of the things
that matter to us,
as we ssttaaammmmmeerrrrr

tooo pppuuttt our
eeexxppperiennccee
intointointowowwwords

and wait
hopefully
for others to
let us know
they understand,

as we read the words describing the ways in which God
has worked in His world,

dying words may
come alive,

new words may
be born,

may
traditional wORds   be used **BUT**
may not

... **THE LIVING CHRIST WILL BE THERE!**

"The present-momentness" of the true and living Word appears whenever the depth in one person's life responds to the depth in another person's life. Then words and experience are wed. ommunication is **COMMUN-ION**. Words are living words.

In the moment in which life touches life, words speak and persons meet.

In the moment in which persons meet and words speak, we know life together.

Then, indeed, we recover persons. Then, indeed, the means of community carry the meaning of becoming genuinely human community.

Then I saw a new heaven and a new earth . . . .
I saw the holy city, new Jerusalem . . . .
    It had . . . twelve gates . . . .
    I saw no temple in the city,
    for its temple is the Lord God . . . .
        Revelation 21:1-22 (RSV)

10
serving: connecting communities

Let's build **III** booths — one each for

MOSES CHRIST ELIJAH

(Luke 9:28-36)

Let's stay right here; let's not listen
to New Being; let's listen to oUrSelves:
    the real is for us
    to enjoy for ourselves!
Let's settle in and stay put.

On a dangerous seacoast where shipwrecks often occur there was once a crude little life-saving station. The building was just a hut, and there was only one boat, but the few devoted members kept a constant watch over the sea, and with no thought for themselves went out day and night tirelessly searching for the lost. Many lives were saved by this wonderful little station, so that it became famous. Some of those who were saved, and various others in the surrounding area, wanted to become associated with the station and give of their time and money and effort for the support of its work. New boats were bought and new crews trained. The little lifesaving station grew.

Some of the members of the lifesaving station were unhappy that the building was so crude and poorly equipped. They felt that a more comfortable place should be provided as the first refuge of those saved from the sea. They replaced the emergency cots with beds and put better furniture in the enlarged building.

Now the lifesaving station became a popular gathering place for its members, and they decorated it beautifully and furnished it exquisitely, because they used it as a sort of club.

Fewer members were now interested in going to sea on lifesaving missions, so they hired lifeboat crews to do this work. The lifesaving motif still prevailed in this club's decoration, and there was a liturgical lifeboat in the room where the club initiations were held.

About this time a large ship was wrecked off the coast, and the hired crews brought in boat loads of cold, wet, and half-drowned people. They were dirty and sick and some of them had black skin and some had yellow skin. The beautiful new club was in chaos. So the property committee immediately had a shower house built outside the club where victims of shipwreck could be cleaned up before coming inside.

At the next meeting, there was a split in the club membership. Most of the members wanted to stop the club's lifesaving activities as being unpleasant and a hindrance to the normal social life of the club. Some members insisted upon lifesaving as their primary purpose and pointed out that they were still called a lifesaving station. But they were finally voted down and told that if they wanted to save the lives of all the various kinds of people who were shipwrecked in those waters, they could begin their own lifesaving station down the coast. They did.

As the years went by, the new station experienced the same changes that had occurred in the old.

It evolved into a club, and yet another lifesaving station was founded. History continued to repeat itself, and if you visit that seacoast today, you will find a number of exclusive clubs along that shore. Shipwrecks are frequent in those waters, but most of the people drown.[65]

Your service you do not know.
>   NOt on this **MOUNTAIN**
>   NOt in **JERUSALEM**

>   Genuine service (rs) will celebrate:
>   **I AM BRINGING INTO BEING**
>   in **SPIRIT** and **TRUTH**

>   (John 4:19-23)

As Bonhoeffer has pointed out, the church (community) is the body of New Humanity <u>when</u> she participates in the sufferings of God by living in this world for the sake of humanity.[66] To live in Christ is to LET others BE.[67] To live in Christ is to exist as His Way.

Genuine ✕-Way links real people in real places with real need. Every part of the community is potentially present to every other part. The mathematics of Community go like this:

>   SERVICE
>   − PRESENCE
>   _____
>   UNREALITY

To the degree there is service without presence, then to that degree we are lost in unreality.

>   PRESENCE
>   − SERVICE
>   _____
>   INGROWNNESS

To the degree there is presence without service, then to that degree we turn in upon ourselves and die.

>   PRESENCE
>   + SERVICE
>   _____
>   COMMUNITY

To the degree all realms and people are potentially present added to the degree we do not end in ourselves, then to that degree we have genuine community.

we make Contact

with our own,
through acts of love;
with our neighbor,
through acts of compassion;
with the stranger,
through acts of justice.

The circle expands from the most immediate human being in our own family to the more removed human being in the family of man to the most remote human being in the family of I AM ALL IN ALL.

When our way becomes Christ's Way, no part is anymore remote nor removed nor immediate than any other part. Unknown strangers turn out to be family.

Look at these faces.
Can you identify who they are?

MY GOD AND MY CHRIST!
(Matthew 25:40)

Familiar family turns out to be stranger.

Who

is

my

family?
(Mark 3:31-33)

WHOEVER DOES THE WILL OF GOD IS MY FAMILY (Mark 3:34-35).

The call of Community, by Community, and for Community scrambles the ordinary meanings of mifyla, gnrhobei, and rtsegnar. Now a stranger is family and family is stranger. Now neighbor is stranger-family and family-stranger. Each and every circumstance calls forth acts of love, acts of compassion, acts of justice.

acts of justice

The complexity of these technologically volcanic times throws up the necessity of structures before people. Individual acts of charity mean little. They perpetuate the illusion of caring while missing the conditions of carefulness. They confuse short-range problems with the long-term predicament. They foster an insidious benevolent paternalism that unintentionally builds oneself up by doing for others what others want and need to do for themselves. In a world like ours, structures alone create and determine widespread justice or injustice.

As never before, we are experiencing "principalities and powers" (Romans 8:38, KJV) — the transpersonal forces that shape and **Shake** and crush and gully persons even before persons have a chance of responding.

Do zoning laws encourage freedom of cultivation by preventing
overcrowding and property neglect

or do the laws allow more
people in less space with
more strain on already
overtaxed facilities?

Does the suburban teenager who
steals hub caps get a greater
chance at "justice"

than the inner city teen-
ager who steals hub caps?

What does a half a loaf of
bread mean in the face of
too many babies?

Is contraceptive help available for the disadvantaged
as well as the advantaged or
are women condemned to endless labor and children cruc-
ified by endless neglect?

To **proclaim** the King-
dom of God is to do battle
with every setting and every
structure which rob people
of their humanity. For Jesus'
ministry meant conflict with
principalities and powers.
Contemporary protest move-
ments — when linked with
organizing community re-
sources — carry on that
exorcising/reconciling work.
The goal is not the elimina-
tion of life but the celebrating
of life, not the doing away
with structures but the
redeeming of

structures, not the spiritualizing of the everyday but the humanizing of the everlasting.[68] The vision of New City as a place of elegance symbolizes the abundant quality of the Way. The glory of divine perfection embraces and transforms the glory of earthly living.

This is no ascetic dualism that views the material world as evil and the spiritual world as good. Rather, here is a majestic vision that the worLd is God's WORLD. The material world is the medium for declaring and disclosing spiritual reality. While no circumstances can either destroy a life of meaning or guarantee it, some circumSTANCES can and do tip the balance. No realm can be excluded from the necessity of our acting justly. Every realm calls for just ordering.

In actuality, Acts of JUSTice tend to be undramatlc. Despite the glamour of prophetic words and despite the excitement of dramatic actions, they concentrate on real change in a desired direction.[69] Rather than asking "where the action is," justice establishes a routine "where the traction is." Instead of marching from one confrontation to another, justice sets up patterns that distribute goods and services fairly and equitably. One's place is secured — a social security number; a guaranteed standard of human living; protection against exploitation; a predictable system of expectations, responsibilities, and rewards.

Independent of anybody's wishes and whims, people know where they stand. They know what they can count on. The rules are there. The decisions have been made. The wheels are in motion.

The skeletal structure of Community determines the justice of the community. By it, firmness is established. By it, uprightness is maintained. By it, growth is possible.

Justice protects people against exploit-
ing powers. Justice staves off people being
ignored. Whether I like it or not,
          children are fed
       mothers are cared for
      housing is available
    education is fostered
work is rewarded.
Whether I like it or not,
people are people!
          Acts of **JUST**ice provide struc-
tures of fairness apart from any particular person or place. These policies, programs, and procedures guarantee a minimum presence of humane and impartial consideration. They deter makers of action from distorting their own importance by what they do for others. They prevent recipients of action from experiencing helpless dependence upon the uncertain gener-
osity of others.[70] A just $ sets life up in terms of uncondition-
al giving rather than disguised getting.

When did we see X and not respond?

If we may never know specifically when we have done justly or loved mercy **(Matthew 25: 34-40)**, nonetheless, there are times when we do know, specifically, the demand to act with compassion. In such moments we are called out of our own life to pass life on to others.

WHO ARE THESE OTHERS?

*A man was once on his way down from Jerusalem to Jericho. He fell into the hands of ban-
dits who stripped off his clothes, beat him up, and left him half dead.*

A Samaritan (Chinese, Vietnamese, Russian, African, Communist) traveler came along to the place wHERE   *the man was lying,*
and at the sight of him HE was tOUCHED with pity. He went across to him and ......
                 and .....
                 and ....
     I went across to him and   ...
                 and   ..
                 and   .

A *neighbor is* ANY one where time IN NEED

Who is neighbor? We are **NeIGH**bor whenever we respond appropriately to need (Luke 10:25-37).

In the midst of war-devastated Moscow, Doctor Zhivago had managed to find a duck and a bottle of vodka. He planned a party for his family. But then the thought hit him:

> . . . their party was a kind of betrayal. You could not imagine anyone in the houses across the street eating or drinking in the same way at the same time. Beyond the windows lay silent, dark, hungry Moscow. Its shops were empty, and as for game and vodka, people had even forgotten to think about such things.[71]

And so it turned out
that only a life similar to the life of those around us, merging with it without a ripple, is genuine life, and that an unshared happiness is not happiness, so that duck and vodka, when they seem to be the only ones in town, are not even duck and vodka.   And this was the most vexing of all.

The community of the gcod Samaritan (Christ's Way) passes sensit**IveNESS** on so others can travel also. Acts are personalized. We no longer live to ourselves; rather we live through ourselves by participating in God's working in his world. Instead of being ruler, cus-tomer, employer, commander, privileged, magistrate,

we are by our presence r e s p o n d e r ,   w a i t e r , s e r v a n t ,   a i d e ,   d o o r m a n ,   e n a b l e r (Philippians 2:3-8). Instead of being worshipped, we witness (Revelation 22:8-9)!

acts of com**PASSiON**

Concrete acts of caring characterize being Christ-to-our-neighbor. Much of the impetus of the growing unity-in-diversity of the ecumenical movement arises from the responses of the church to the cry of Community. In explaining the "Life and Work" emphasis of the Stockholm Conference in 1925, Archbishop Nathan Soderblom told of an old farmer who had visited him. The farmer pointed out, "Archbishop, Christendom is entering a new phase. The Church of the Priest has been and is over — Rome. The Church of the Levite has come in its place — Wittenberg [Luther] and Geneva [Calvin]. Now it is over and the Church of the Good Samaritan is beginning." [72]

The Community we proclaim is ultimately a unity of shared purpose more than of single past. Now we are caught up in a unity going beyond dogma. Now we are empowered by a unity beyond church gOVERnMENt. Now we are servants of a unity that would heal the nations so that I AM beCOMEs all IN ALL (Revelation 21–22).

$$\frac{\text{acts of justice} + \text{acts of compassion}}{\text{ActS of LOVE}}$$

The space gap between young/old, have/have-nots, family/stranger is bridged by living love. We are ministered to even as we minister. Mutual caring and mutual sharing. The ideal of a middle-class mold misses the heart of the matter. Each group, any person, every culture has something of worth necessary to establishing, maintaining, and enhancing our humanity. [73]

"We know that we have crossed the frontier from death to life because we do love our brothers . . .

God is love,
and the man whose life is lived
in love

does, in fACT, live in God,
and God does, in fACT, live
in him.

YEs, we love GOd BEcause He first LOVEd us."

(1 John 3:14-18; 4:16, 19-20, Phillips [Underscoring and bold face are author's])

By faith Abraham obeyed when he was called
to go out. . . .

11
the trip

Our response to being in the community of the
WORLD and in the world of comm**UNITY** is to set out to discover
what it is like and to share in what it might become. Rather
than tuning out, we turn on. Instead of holding back, we take
off. We are called to be in this world as travelers. Freed from
everything, we are free for humanity. An exciting adventure
lies before us.

But the trouble with traveling these days is the chaos
in transportation. Roads are torn up. Maps are quickly out-
of-date. Cities and countries convulse with crises. How can we
travel when we lack sure ways of getting around? Is there a
Way appropriate both to faith and to our situation? Is there
a **WAY** both to be Christ's Way and to become ╳ 's Way?

Abraham stands out as the representative trip taker
for people-of-faith. As such he provides an orienting image to
understand and to incarnate concrete faithfulness. He unfolds
a way of being Highway of our God.

We cannot not take a trip. Whether we want to or
not we travel. Even when we stay put, we are on the road — to
the past. Everyone is called to go out.

CALLed to TAKE a TRIP

By faIth
AbrahAM obeyed when he was
cALLed to go out to a place which
he was to receive as an inHEritaNCE . . .

To the literal minded that refers to a man named Abraham packing up and moving from Ur of the Chaldeans across the fertile crescent down into Egypt and back up into Canaan. A family migrates — so what? It happens all the time — all the time — all the time — all the. . . .

To the faith-minded, that migration discloses the people-of-God. Movement in space is not so much the issue as movement in spirit. We are uprooted to travel through life as persons instead of staying in place as things. We leave the past to **be** in the pre**sent** for the sake of a future.

I AM COMMUNITY-IN-DIVERSITY
you ARE community-in-diversity
THEREFORE
YOU (plural/singular) BE
COMMUNITY-IN-DIVERSITY

THE SummONs *We are/become*
to answer
COMES *the human community*   we are answerable!

THE deMANd
to respond *we truly are* we <u>are</u> responsible!
APPEARS

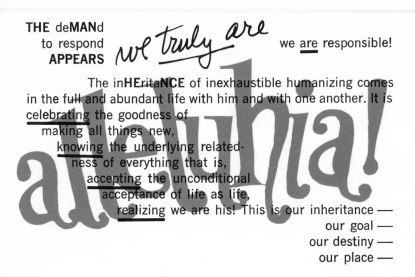

The inHEritaNCE of inexhaustible humanizing comes
in the full and abundant life with him and with one another. It is
celebrating the goodness of
making all things new,
knowing the underlying relatedness of everything that is,
accepting the unconditional
acceptance of life as life,
realizing we are his! This is our inheritance —
our goal —
our destiny —
our place —

But to be called forth as I AM's PEOPLE raises the
question of traveling even more keenly. How are we to travel?
What is to be our style of getting about?

By faith Abraham obeyed UN Cert**AI**N**T**Y
when he was called to go out
to a place which he was to receive
as an inheritance; and he went out not knowing where he was to go

Even though called to joyful fulfillment, we can never
be sure what we are about — what human community is or
where human community is or when human community is.
All we know is it **SOME**how **IS**. No map keeps us on route.
No guidebook gives sure directions.

He who lives must perpetually
begin anew,
perpetually risk all,
and therefore
his truth is
not a having but a becoming.

"The person who knows direction responds with the
whole of his being to each new situation with no
other preparation than
his presence
and
his readiness to respond." [74]

The historian sees history as turning points made up of chance and accident as well as calculated planning. Under and within and beyond all events, however, people-of-faith perceive the moving power of I AM INEXHAUSTIBLE HUMAN-IZING. The community-in-diversity claims:

> God is in the midst of this moment.
> With him every point is a turning
> point. No point is so removed that
> it cannot lead directly to him.

>> We do not know where we are going or
>> how we are going when we set out. In
>> any immediate moment we are uncertain
>> of what we are about, yet we are cer-
>> tain it is he who is calling us to the
>> responsible life.

Within today's events we know there are possibilities. If we listen without distorting, then we do find new meaning waiting to be born. Our style makes us confident of meaning-ful possibility. The trip takes us and carries us along in spite of ourselves. When we would control its course, we destroy its promise. When we give ourselves to its possibilities, we receive its blessings.

*By faith
Abraham obeyed when he was called to go out to a place
which he was to receive as an inheritance;
and he went out not knowing where he was to go.
By faith
he traveled in the land of promise* as in a foreign land

Reality is hard. If our style leaves us uncertain be-cause we never know specifically where we are going, it breeds uncomfortableness because we seldom are sure exactly where we are. The passage implies Abraham lived in the land of ful-fillment as a stranger, a foreigner, an alien, an outsider. Even in New City, the PlACE is unfamiliar.

We are outsiders to culture as well as to church. For we never see God's People clearly and confidently in any specific situation. **EVER**y structure is po**TENT**ially recognizable as the sp**HERE** in which he works. No structure finally and definitely discloses everything. Each event, when it is encountered, opens an abyss of mystery. Too rapid an adaptation in which we lose uncomfortableness causes us to strangle possibility (cf. Hebrews 13:9).

> "The whole middle class church tends to be such a closely bound fellowship that church and social relations are synonymous. The very groups which first dispersed with the ranks and privileges of the world in the name of a close koinonia have become — ironically, precisely, because of their emphasis on fellowship — the worst examples in our society of the conformity to the ranks and standards of the world." [75]

While genuine Reality within the midst of passing flux is seldom easy to discern, nevertheless, that Reality is the place toward which we are directed.

By faith
Abraham obeyed when he was called to go out to a place
which he was to receive as an inheritance;

> *and he went out not knowing*
> *where he was to go.*

By faith
he traveled in the promised land as in a foreign land,
living in tents.

unsettled

Again, the unexpected: living-in-tents — no permanence, no settling down, no digging in. In contrast to a building, a tent signifies mobility, uprootedness, flexibility. It can be put up or taken down with little effort. We are community-on-the-move.

The unsettledness, however, is not necessarily physical dislocation. We must be quite clear about that. Living-in-tents-on-the-move is not literal but symbolic. It means keeping life **Fresh and Open**

Harvey Cox has pointed out that, in their life in Canaan, the Jews experienced a traumatic clash between Yahweh and the Baalim, the recognized deities of the land. The word "baal" refers to "possessor" or "inhabitant." The baalim, consequently, were the **PROP**rietor**S** of various activities, especially of particular towns and places. In effect, they were "immobile gods . . . the gods of a sedentary people who were suspicious of any kind of change." [76]

Contrariwise, YHWH is a mobile god. He frees people from special places. He wipes out special classes. His Community travels. He presents an open world.

The Community-on-the-road takes many forms. It may be the house church movement in England where early in the morning a minister goes to the home of a parishioner and there around the breakfast table a few neighbors gather to discuss work, to share concerns, to break bread, to drink wine, to praise God. It may be a small luncheon on Wall Street where financiers gather to talk about what is happening to them and how their faith matters in what they are doing.

It may be a picket line singing, "Deep in my heart, I do believe, we shall overcome someday." It may be a coffeehouse near the university where a play is read, a poem recited, a combo blares, and god is rejected. It may be an inner-city store front (church) where the dispossessed know someone listens; someone cares; someone fights for cleaner toilets, fewer rats, better schools, stabler famil It may be a church mortgaging its property to invest in low income housing.

It may be a hospital where a nurse unburdens to a chaplain her fears of death as she cares for a woman her own age dying of breast cancer.

Community-on-the-move threatens the status quo. It questions established power. It triggers social change. Wherever life is on the line — whether in slum or suburb, in industry or education, in hospitals or housing, in Congress or the United Nations, abroad or at home — the power of becoming Community is at work (Luke 17:20-21).

> Research in small groups shows that the longer the life of any particular leadership, the less open and less free the group becomes and probably the less efficient the group is in solving new problems.[77]

They died in faith not having received what was promised.

INcomplete — no **FULL**ness, no wholeness, no de-**LIGHT, NO** joy, no **COMMUNITY**! Uncertain! Uncomfortable! Unsettled! What kind of style is that????

Here we confront the strange mystery of the **PEO-PLE**-for-others **GO**d style. It is open-ended. No matter how much we do, there is still more to be done. No matter what we are, there is still more to be/come. Every action releases new possibilities. **NEW** hu**MAN**ity has already come — but — not yet . . . . . . I AM COMING

soon . . .

(Revelation 22:20)

We see the promises in the distance. We hail them as true. We are convinced of their reality. So we travel. We fix our e**YES** on genuine community. We long for the truer life of Community than the pale caricature in community.

It is not easy to maintain a creative tension between being called out from the world and being sent to the world. We can get so caught up with not being of the world that we end up not being in the world. On the other hand, we can get so caught up with being in the world that we end up being of the world.

The vision shows we are to be in the world as fools — free from pretense, free from fear, free from ourselves, free from each other (1 Corinthians 4:9-13), free to be for others —— in ways that matter genuinely, fools for Christ's sake (Galatians 5:13-14).

Within the church (Community) focus is on becoming genuine highWay. We must ask ourselves: what does it mean to be Community in which respect and trust and responsibility are present?

Within the (Church) community focus is on all people becoming authentic human Community. We must ask ourselves: what does it mean for respect and trust and responsibility to be present everywhere — at work, in the home, on the street, among the nations?

The style of faithfulness is so much fuller and richer and vaster than anything we sense in our here-and-now. Little wonder we experience restlessness luring us on to the larger life.

Yes, we have our hopes, we make our plans, we carry out our purposes in terms of <u>our own</u> understanding of coming fulfillment. Yet, all our anticipations are but vague images of the more genuine life that is a-comin'.

Time has "an offspring in her womb we cannot even fancy." That offspring is waiting to be born each day through each person within each community for each place: in us but never from us, through us but never ending in us.

There is a story told of Leonardo da Vinci that in the first painting of the "Last Supper" he put such detail into two cups standing on the table that a friend, seeing them, stared in open-mouth amazement. Thereupon the artist seized a brush and with one sweep of his hand painted them out of the picture, crying, "Not that! That isn't what I want you to see! It's the face. Look at the face!" [78]

If you recall that painting, you remember the way all lines move from the outside inward and converge on the face of Christ. Every line directs us to him. No detail of cup or window or person is allowed to distract from that center. Yet every line likewise leads away from that center to the outside. From <u>the</u> man to <u>every</u> man.

Just as the Lord Christ is set apart from the world and also sent to the world, even so the people-of-God are to be/come PEOPLE that all people might come to know themselves as PEOPLE.

I AM COMING

COME,
GENUINE COMMUNITY,
COME!

notes

[1] Karl Barth, *Evangelical Theology: An Introduction* (New York: Holt, Rinehart & Winston, 1963), p. 37.

[2] From "I Am a Rock" by Paul Simon. © 1965, Charing Cross Music. Used with permission.

[3] Marshall McLuhan, *Understanding Media* (New York: Signet Books, 1966), p. ix.

[4] *Ibid.*, p. 56.

[5] Clyde Kluckhohn, "Have There Been Discernible Shifts in American Values During the Past Generation?" In Elting E. Morison, ed., *The American Style: Essays in Value and Performance* (New York: Harper & Row, Publishers, 1958), p. 207.

[6] See J. C. Hoekendijk, *The Church Inside Out*, ed. L. A. Hoedemaker and Pieter Tijmes, trans. Isaac C. Rottenberg (Philadelphia: The Westminster Press, 1966).

[7] See Will Herberg, *Protestant—Catholic—Jew: An Essay in American Religious Sociology* (Garden City, N.Y.: Doubleday & Co., 1956), pp. 186-213.

[8] See Gerhard Lenski, *The Religious Factor: A Sociological Study of Religion's Impact on Politics, Economics, and Family Life* (Garden City, N.Y.: Doubleday & Co., 1961).

[9] Bernard Berelson and Gary A. Steiner, eds., *Human Behavior: An Inventory of Scientific Findings* (New York: Harcourt, Brace & World, 1964), pp. 183-184. Adapted from Leonard Carmichael, H. P. Logan, and A. A. Walter, "An Experimental Study of the Effect of Language on the Reproduction of Visually Perceived Form," *Journal of Experimental Psychology*, vol. 15 (1932), pp. 73-86.

[10] Helen Keller, *The Story of My Life* (New York: Grosset & Dunlap, 1904), p. 287.

[11] Robert Frost, *Complete Poems of Robert Frost* (New York: Holt, Rinehart, & Winston, 1964), p. 575.

[12] See *The Interpreter's Dictionary of the Bible* (Nashville: Abingdon Press, 1962), "E-J," pp. 407-417, and "K-Q," pp. 500-508.

[13] Erich Fromm, *You Shall Be as Gods* (New York: Holt, Rinehart & Winston, 1966), p. 31.

[14] See *The Interpreter's Dictionary of the Bible, op. cit.*, "K-Q," pp. 663-668.

[15] Harvey Cox, *The Secular City* (New York: The Macmillan Company, 1965), p. 134.

[16] Haim G. Ginott, *Group Psychotherapy with Children* (New York: McGraw-Hill Book Co., 1961), p. 6.

[17] Walter Lowrie, *A Short Life of Kierkegaard* (Garden City, N.Y.: Doubleday & Co., 1961), p. 71.

[18] P. T. Forsyth, *Positive Preaching and the Modern Mind* (New York: Eaton & Mains, 1907), p. 174.

[19] Lawrence Ferlinghetti, *A Coney Island of the Mind* (New York: New Directions Books, 1958), p. 88.

[20] Martin Luther King, Jr., *Stride Toward Freedom* (New York: Harper & Row, Perennial Library, 1964), pp. 61-62.

[21] Henry Bettenson, ed. and trans., "Irenaeus" in *The Early Christian Fathers* (London: Oxford University Press, 1958), p. 106.

[22] *Look*, July 27, 1965, pp. 30-34, 38-40.

[23] Truman Capote, *The Grass Harp* (New York: The New American Library, 1951), p. 42.

[24] *Time*, July 30, 1965, p. 16.

[25] Drawn and interpreted by Richard Fears. Used with permission.

[26] Carl R. Rogers, *On Becoming a Person* (Boston: Houghton Mifflin Company, 1961), p. 25.

[27] Romola Nijinsky, ed., *The Diary of Vaslav Nijinsky* (New York: Simon and Schuster, Inc., 1936), p. 184.

[28] See Bernhard W. Anderson, *Understanding the Old Testament* (Englewood Cliffs, N.J.: Prentice-Hall, 1957), pp. 160-182.

[29] Ralph Ellison, *Invisible Man* (New York: Random House, 1952), p. 3.

[30] See Kenneth B. Clark, *Dark Ghetto: Dilemmas of Social Power* (New York: Harper & Row, Publishers, 1965), pp. 223-240.

[31] Albert H. van den Heuvel, *The Humiliation of the Church* (Philadelphia: The Westminster Press, 1966), p. 41.

[32] Eugen Rosenstock-Huessy, *The Christian Future or The Modern Mind Outrun* (New York: Charles Scribner's Sons, 1946), pp. 117-118.

[33] Cited by John Hutchison, *Faith, Reason, and Existence* (New York: Oxford University Press, 1956), p. 84.

[34] For a fuller discussion of these ways of relating, see Alan Keith Lucas, "The Nature of the Healing Process," *The Christian Scholar*, Summer, 1960, pp. 119-127; Karen Horney, *Our Inner Conflicts* (New York: W. W. Norton & Co., 1945); and Carl R. Rogers, *op. cit.*

[35] I am indebted to Mr. Dominick Masucci of the New York State Department of Transportation for insight into the nature and meaning of transportation.

[36] William Golding, *Lord of the Flies* (New York: Coward-McCann, Inc., 1954, 1955), pp. 56, 90-91, 109. Used with permission.

[37] Reuel Howe, *Man's Need and God's Action* (Greenwich, Conn.: The Seabury Press, 1953), p. 24.

[38] Dietrich Bonhoeffer, *Letters and Papers from Prison* (New York: The Macmillan Company, 1962), pp. 222-223.

[39] *The Interpreter's Dictionary of the Bible, op. cit.*, "A-D," pp. 607-616.

[40] Dietrich Bonhoeffer, *Ethics*, ed. Eberhard Bethge (New York: The Macmillan Company, 1955), pp. 20-21.

[41] Solon T. Kimball and James E. McClellan, Jr., *Education and the New America* (New York: Random House, 1962), p. 6.

[42] *The New York Times*, December 31, 1967, p. E-7.

[43] Stephen C. Rose, *Renewal*, October-November, 1965, p. 5.

[44] Erich Fromm, *Man for Himself* (New York: Holt, Rinehart & Winston, 1947), p. 209.

[45] Rosenstock-Huessy, *op. cit.*, p. 137.

[46] Lawrence Ferlinghetti, *op. cit.*, p. 49.

[47] Dag Hammarskjold, *Markings* (New York: Alfred A. Knopf, 1964), p. 67.

[48] Rosenstock-Huessy, *op. cit.*, p. 114.

[49] *Ibid.*, pp. 113-131.

[50] Jurgen Moltmann, *Theology of Hope* (London: SCM Press, 1967), p. 285.

[51] Forsyth, *op. cit.*

[52] Hendrick Kraemer, *A Theology of the Laity* (Philadelphia: The Westminster Press, 1958), p. 176.

[53] See Hendrick Kraemer, *The Communication of the Christian Faith* (Philadelphia: The Westminster Press, 1956).

[54] Edward Steichen as quoted in *The Family of Man* (New York: Museum of Modern Art, 1955), p. 23.

[55] See Sidney Jourard, *The Transparent Self* (Princeton: D. Van Nostrand, Inc., 1964).

[56] Ugo Betti, *Three Plays: The Queen and the Rebels; The Burnt Flower; Bud: Summertime*, ed. and trans. Henry Reed (New York: Grove Press, 1958), p. 151. I am indebted to Marjorie Matthews for this reference.

[57] Robert Bretall, ed., *A Kierkegaard Anthology* (Princeton: Princeton University Press, 1951), pp. 28, 100.

[58] Jourard, *op. cit.*, p. 16.

[59] Simone Weil, *Waiting for God*, trans. Emma Crawford (New York: G. P. Putnam's Sons, 1951), p. 27.

[60] Anatol Rapoport, *Operational Philosophy: Integrating Knowledge and Action* (New York: Harper & Row, Publishers, 1953), pp. 4-5.

[61] Reuel Howe, *The Miracle of Dialogue* (Greenwich, Conn.: The Seabury Press, 1963), p. 23.

[62] For a more systematic exploration of ways we withdraw from contact and ways we can contact each other, see Everett L. Shostrom, *Man, the Manipulator: The Inner Journey from Manipulation to Actualization* (New York: Bantam Books, 1968).

[63] Rogers, *op. cit.*, p. 332.

[64] Eberhard Mueller, founder of the Evangelical Academy at Bad Boll, Germany. Cited by Franklin H. Littell, *Pastoral Psychology*, December, 1964, p. 9.

[65] Theodore Wedel, "Evangelism—the Mission of the Church to Those Outside